Evolution of Employment Law and Practice

Philip Benjamin

Copyright © 2015 Philip Benjamin

All rights reserved, including the right to reproduce this book, or portions thereof in any form. No part of this text may be reproduced, transmitted, downloaded, decompiled, reverse engineered, or stored, in any form or introduced into any information storage and retrieval system, in any form or by any means, whether electronic or mechanical without the express written permission of the author.

ISBN: 978-1-326-20381-8

Chapter 1 – The employment relationship	1
Chapter 2 – Mutual Trust and Confidence	12
Chapter 3 – The European perspective (TUPE)	28
Chapter 4 – The European perspective (ECHR)	39
Chapter 5 – Collective employment rights	57
Chapter 6 – Discrimination	70
Chapter 7 - Termination of employment	97
Chapter 8 – Evolution of the employment tribunal system	109
Chapter 9 – Composition of employment tribunals	117
Chapter 10 – Settlement agreements	126
Chapter 11 – Conclusion	131
Bibliography	134

Preface

In recent years there have been numerous developments in employment law. An area of law which was originally easy to understand has evolved into a highly complex and legalistic discipline.

This book endeavours to provide an analysis of the evolutionary nature of employment law. It also attempts to provide a bridge between the academic study of employment law and its practical application. Catering for a range of learning styles, this book outlines the evolution of the main principles underpinning the legal system in this area. It is hoped that the book will provide the reader with a good understanding of the more important components of employment law and the process that has led to the employment regime in existence today.

I would like to express my gratitude to several people for the support that I have received in preparing this edition. First to Madeleine and our two boys, Adam and Alex, for allowing me the time to do this. Secondly, to my colleagues at Regent's University London and also to the students on my law modules. I greatly value their support and practical assistance.

Whilst every attempt has been made to ensure that the information contained in this book is correct, no warranty, express or implied is given as to its accuracy. No liability is accepted for any error or omission. The information contained in this book is not advice to any reader and may not be taken as a definitive statement of the law. Whenever an issue arises as to the engagement of a specific employment and/or discrimination related matter, obligation or right, then the reader is recommended to seek appropriate individual legal advice from a suitably qualified legal practitioner who has been formally instructed in connection with the matter.

March 2015

Chapter 1 – The Employment Relationship

UK law has traditionally focused on the relationship between employer and employee. As a result, the majority of employment rights apply to employees only. Consequently, workers who work under a contract of services have enjoyed the benefit of these rights, and those workers who perform a contract for services have been excluded.

Section 230(1) Employment Rights Act 1996 defines an employee as 'an individual who has entered into a works under a contract of employment'. This Section goes onto define a 'contract of employment' as a contract of service or apprenticeship. No definition is given to a contract of service, and consequently explanatory recourse must be had to the common law for judicial determination.

UK employment law is increasingly influenced by the implementation of European Union Directives. As a result, there is a range of new employment rights that apply to a larger group called 'workers'. It is increasingly common to find the term 'worker' appearing in Directives and indeed section 23 ERA 1999 specifically confers upon the Secretary of State by order, the power to extend statutory employment rights to workers other than employees.

The additional importance of distinguishing between an employee and a 'worker' is that there are several statutory rights given to workers which would include those providing work and services under either a contract for services or a contract of service. Examples of statutory rights extent to trade union membership, whistle blowers and part-time workers.

As a general rule, those who are self employed and are in business to provide a client or customer with professional or other services are not workers. There are advantages to both parties in the employment relationship of such an arrangement. A self employed contractor can argue that he should be responsible for tax under Schedule D which has a more generous deduction and allowance entitlement than Schedule E.

It is also arguable that the self employment relationship allows for a greater flexibility in the market place, as an employer will be able to pick and choose who and when he requires services from a pool of available self employed contractors.

Nevertheless, parliament has long recognised that excessive flexibility in the market place can be to the detriment of workers' rights.

In 1970 the Committee of Safety & Health at Work was setup under the chairmanship of Lord Robens. This recognised the problems of the self employed worker who was at that time not entitled to the benefits of work place safety legislation. In his review of the Robens report, R.W Howells noted the inherent unfairness with which the legal system appeared to perpetuate a distinction between the employed and self employed. This had the result that too much effort had been wasted in demarcation matters remote from the business of accident reduction.

The Robens report lead eventually to the Health & Safety at Work Act 1974. However, even today employers must adopt a higher standard of care towards their employees than towards independent contractors who work for them.

It should also be noted that parliament has given rights to employees alone. Principally s94 of the Employments Rights Act 1996 provides employees with a remedy for unfair dismissal. Section 135 provides for payments on redundancy. These rights are not available to the self employed worker.

Once a contract for service has been established, then in addition to the expressed terms of the contract, the courts are prepared to imply certain terms into the employment relationship, in circumstances where no express provision has been made.

Principally, there is an implied term that the employer will treat its employee in a reasonable manner as part of the duty to preserve the relationship of mutual trust and confidence. This means that the employer will not, without reasonable and proper cause, conduct himself in a manner calculated or likely to destroy or seriously damage the relationship of trust and confidence which should exist between him and the employee.

In Malik v Bank of Credit & Commerce International (1997) ICR 606, the employer bank went into liquidation after having operated for sometime in a corrupt and dishonest manner. The court held that this conduct amounted to a breach of the implied contractual obligation of mutual trust and confidence, as the employees employment prospects were tainted by the employer's reputation.

Similarly, in French v Barclays Bank Plc (1998) IRLR 646, the adoption of mutual trust and confidence was applied in circumstances where the employee had been directed to move across country by his employer and had been initially granted a relocation allowance. The allowance was then withdrawn when the employer had difficulty in selling his house, and as a consequence he was forced to sell his house at a lower value. The court upheld the employees claim for breach of contract in respect of the shortfall, on the grounds that the employer had breached the duty of mutual trust by going back on its original agreement to advance the allowance.

Other common law implied terms flowing from a contract of employment relate to an implied term to pay agreed wages, and an implied obligation to provide work in certain circumstances. In the case of William Hill Organisation Ltd v Tucker (1998) IRLR 313, the employee was a senior spread betting dealer within the organization. His contract expressed the imposing obligation on him to work those hours necessary to carry out his duties. When the employee resigned without given the required notice period, his employers wanted to put him on garden leave although it had no expressed right to do so. The court held that the employee's special skills required frequent exercise, and therefore placing the employee on garden leave was a breach of the employee's obligation to provide work during the employment, including the notice period.

Another distinction is relevant to the doctrine of vicarious liability whereby employers are liable for the negligence of their employees during the normal course of employment. Conversely, employers are not usually responsible for the torts of their independent contractors.

This has a knock on effect in respect of the level of premium payable by the employer or indemnity insurance – an issue especially relevant to the building industry.

As a consequence of the importance of defining the distinction between a worker and independent contractor, the common law has adopted several different tests of employment status.

The traditional test was one of control. This test assesses the extent to which a person is under the direction and control of another party. Attention is given to the manner in which the work is done. As a general rule, the greater the degree of control, the more likely it is that a contract of service has come into existence.

In Walker v Crystal Palace FC 1910 KB 87 the applicant was a football player who although had some freedom of action, was held to be under the control of his captain. His employers right to control was held to be the determining factor in establishing a contract of service.

Conversely in Hitchcock v Post Office 1980 ICR 100 the applicant ran a sub post office as part of a shop he owned. Although the post office exercised control of many of his activities, it was held that this was because of the need to ensure financial control, rather than being a control of managerial functions. On this basis, the applicant was not held to be an employee of the post office.

Under the control test, if an employer can tell the employee not only what to do, but also how to do it, then a contract of service exists. The main problem with this test is that the employer is viewed of having superior skill and knowledge. This is clearly inappropriate. In modern conditions an employee maybe highly skilled and qualified to the extent that the employer is unable to instruct the employee on how the work should be done.

The control test is not dead, but modern decisions tend to utilise it as one of several tests in determining the employment relationship. The issue of the right to control appears to be the more modern view and the greater the degree of control, the more likely it will be that the contract is one of service. The control test also allows for a degree of delegation, so long as this is not inconsistent with the right to control.

In MacFarlane v Glasgow City Council 2001 IRLR 7 the applicant was a gymnastic instructor working for the local authority on a casual basis. She was held to be an employee even though she could send a substitute teacher, because here, the substitute had to be from a list of instructors approved by the local authority, which itself organized the replacement and paid them directly. Of crucial importance, was the fact that the local authority paid the employee direct and as a consequence the EAT was able to distinguish the existing decision of Ready Mixed Concrete (South East) Ltd.

An alternative test is that of integration. This considers the nature of the employment by the employee. If the employee is fully integrated into the organisation, then there is more likely to be a contract of service.

The integration test has certain advantages, particularly in relation to skilled employees who are integrated into the organisation.

In Cassidy v Minister of Health 1951 to KB 343 the Court held that a medical practitioner was sufficiently integrated into his organisation so as to give rise to a contract of employment. The fact that the employees skill was greater than that of his employer did not defeat the reality of his employment.

However, the main problem with the integration test, is that although it is useful in clarifying the employment status of professional and managerial workers, it is less effective in dealing with the position of workers employed by a sub contractor of the employer's business. Such workers may be integral to the employers business, but not necessarily employees. As a result, the common law has developed a further multiple test which includes the issues of economic reality and mutuality of obligation.

The economic reality test recognises that it is a combination and balance of features that matters more than one simple check list. Consequently, all these factors for and against the presence of an employment relationship are put into balance. Two key questions are then posed;
1. If the worker is in business on his own account.
2. Is there a mutual obligation to provide work and perform tasks as directed.

In determining whether the worker is in business on his own account, the tribunal will look at all the surrounding features to the relationship. This is due to payment of wages, income tax, power to dismiss and holidays. The tribunal will also look as to which party is taking on a financial risk and who is sharing the profits. In Ready Mix Concrete (South East) Ltd the minister of pensions 1968 2QB 497, the applicant lorry drivers had to obey a wide range of company rules. Although they owned their lorries and maintained them at their own expense, they had to sell them back to the company at an agreed price. The applicant paid there own tax and national insurance contributions. Also, and unlike the situation in the MacFarlane Case ante, the lorry drivers were not paid direct. The court held that the lorry drivers were self employed. Of crucial importance in this case was the fact that the drivers could with the company consent, arranged for a substitute driver to do their job. However, this was not the only factor that the court took into account, and all the other circumstances of the relationship tended towards a contract for services.

The tribunal will take into account the intentions of the parties in determining the existence of a contract of employment, particularly where both parties agree to the relationship being a contract for services. However, an express clause in the contract is not conclusive, and inequality in bargaining power between the parties maybe an important factor.

In Davies v New England College of Arundel 1977 ICR 6, the applicant was a self employed college lecturer. He described himself as self employed and both parties acknowledged self employed status. However, when dismissed, he claimed unfair dismissal. The EAT held that the applicant was an employee of the college, after having taken into account the economic reality of his position within the organisation.

In determining whether there is a mutual obligation to provide work and perform tasks, those parties to the contract must be under an irreducible minimum of obligations. This must amount to one party providing work, usually for a remuneration, and the other exercising efficient control over the other party who must personally perform the work required.

In Carmichael v National Power Plc 2000 IRLR 43, the applicant worked as a tour guide on a casual basis. She worked as and when required, but she was not obliged to take the work. There was no guarantee that the work would be available. When she did work, tax and national insurance were deducted. The House of Lords held that she was not an employee – there was no obligation on the company to provide work and she was not obliged to take it. There was therefore an absence of the irreducible minimum of mutual obligations necessary to show a contract of employment.

A different approach was taken in Nethermere of St Neots v Gardiner and Taverna 1984 ICR 612. In this case, the applicants were home workers who largely regulated their own work load. Nevertheless, it was noted that the applicant had a long standing relationship with their employer and did the same type of work as their full time equivalent. They were held to be employees under a contract of service as their employment was so regular and constant that an irreducible minimum of obligations on each party had come into existence.

The contract that had arisen in the St Neots Case is an example of an 'umbrella' contract of employment which took into account the totality of all the individual assignments that had been undertaken by the employee over a course of time. In such situations, continuity is presumed to run from the beginning of the first assignment and there will be no gaps in the employment relationship when the employee is not working between assignments.

It is suggested that the Carmichael and Nethermere Cases are far from satisfactory in providing a practical solution in determining the existence of a contract of employment.

Using this analysis, it is conceivable for there to be a series of short term lower level contracts, for short bursts of employment, which will although going on for a period of over one year, would not in themselves add up to providing the worker with the necessary qualifying period in order to put him within the Statutory framework from employment protection.

The status of workers employed via an employment agency is one which has given rise to the significant litigation in recent years. In this situation, the agency enters into a contract with both the employee worker and the client company. The worker will do work for the client company, but generally the employment relationship is with the agency.

However, in certain circumstances where the agency worker is in long term employment, it maybe possible for an agency worker to be an employee of either the agency or the client company.

In Motorola Ltd v Davidson & Melville Craig Group 2001 IRLR 4, the applicant had worked for Motorola as an agency worker supplied by the agency Melville Craig Group. The agency did not just send any agency worker to Motorola – as the client company had to agree the service of each worker. The applicant terms and conditions were set down by the agency, but he worked directly under the instructions of Motorola and was treated the same as any full time employee. He worked exclusively at Motorola for two years before being dismissed. EAT took into account the reality of the circumstances, the length of employment and the degree of control. The EAT found that there was an employment contract between the applicant and Motorola.

This line was developed in Franks v Reuters Ltd 2003 IRLR 423, where the worker had worked at the client companies premises for a period of nearly six years uninterrupted service. The Court held that the period of employment was important but not a conclusive factor in determining whether a contractual relationship between the worker and the client company had come into existence.

The leading case in this area used to be that of Dacas v Brookstreet Bureau (UK) Ltd 2004 IRLR 359. In this case, the applicant was a cleaner registered with the employment agency, Brookstreet Bureau. Their agreement stated that the relationship would not give rise to a contract of employment either with the agency or/and client company. The agency was responsible for discipline and pay, where as the client company had exclusive day to day control and could decide when it no longer wanted the applicant. Mrs Dacas had been signed to the client company for six years until it asked for her to be withdrawn. The court held that the agency was not the applicant's employer, as it was not obliged to provide Mrs Dacas with work, and it did not have sufficient control over her. However, the court went on to hold that she was employed by the client company and that the express wording of her contract with the agency did not override this. It was possible for the express obligations between Mrs Dacas and the agency to be read across a triangular relationship between Mrs Dacas, the agency and the client company. Consequently, such obligation could be inserted into an implied contract between Mrs Dacas and the client company.

In reality, Mrs Dacas did not derive any practical benefit from the House of Lords decision, as she failed to cross-appeal against the EAT's earlier judgment. However, the principals set out by the House of Lords in its decision are of application to future cases.

Reference used to be made to the Conduct of Employment Agencies and Employment Business Regulations 2003. This lays out detailed rules on the provision of contractual documents as between all parties, including whether the worker is to be an employee of the employment agency 'employment business' or, a contact for services. However, even if the worker is expressly described as self employed, this will not exclude the possibility of a contract of service coming into existence pursuant to the Dacas principal.

In Royal National Lifeboat Institution v Bushawa 2005 IRLR 674 there was a written agreement between an employment agency and a worker which described her as a temporary worker engaged under a contract for services. The EAT held that it was entitled to go behind the written agreement and look at the reality of the situation to determine whether the contract was in truth a contract of employment.

Research into office temps revealed that whereas most employment agencies preferred an exclusive and long term relationship, client companies stress the benefits of multiple providers in order to 'keep the agencies on their toes'. It was also noted that client companies expected referred workers to possess relevant office skills and they were not prepared to assist in terms of training or integration with existing employees. The general mutual expectation was one of transience.

It is therefore submitted that the issue with regard to the status of an employee employed by an employment agency is unsatisfactory not only with regard to common law definition, but also taking into account the expectations of the parties that generally enter into this type of arrangement. One could suggest that the tribunal should take into account not only expectations of the parties at the time the employee initially commenced employment, but also the intentions which subsequently develop over a period of time; ie, did the parties originally intend a contract of service?

Conversely, it is submitted that a client company should not be entitled to avoid a contractual relationship with the employee, purely because none was originally intended. Had the applicant in Dacas been a model employee from the point of the client company, then it is arguable that the client company would have eventually had to pay a separate agency fee to the employment agency, in order to convert the temporary employee to permanent status within the client companies' organisations.

So far, in determining whether or not an employment relationship exists, we have looked at the various approaches taken by the common law. These have included the control test, integration test and the concept of economic reality. Each one of these tests does not provide clarity in the determination of identifying an employee.

Even where all three approaches have been utilized, different outcomes can arise where the facts are only marginally different. An example of this, are the MacFarlene and Readymixed Concrete cases. These cases had similar facts but the courts determined different outcomes.

The National Minimum Wage Act 1988 and National Minimum Wage Regulations have set down statutory rules relating to the payment of wages, and in particular establish a National Minimum Wage.

Section 1 of the Act defines a 'worker' as an individual who has entered into or works under either a contract of employment or a contract whereby he or she 'undertakes to do or perform personally any work or services for another party to the contract who's status is not by virtue of the contract that of a client or customer of any profession or business undertaking carried on by the individual'. The Act thereby adopts a wider definition of 'worker'. Indeed, the Act appears to recognize that its definition of worker would encompass a larger body of employees than that which would be included at common law. Consequently, the Act recognizes that an 'agency worker' might not come within the definition because of the absence of a contractual relationship between the employee and either the agency and/or the client company.

Similarly the Working Time Regulations 1998 were in acted in order to regularise the extent of working time controls protecting the working population in general, subject only to specific derogations. The regulations arose as a result of implementing EU Directives. Regulation 2(i) defines a 'worker' which is similar to the definition given in the National Minimum Wage regulations ante.

It can be seen that recent statutory and regulatory standards by utilising the more up to date definition of 'worker' have the intention of enabling a broader class of persons to be captured by employment relations. This would not have been the case had the narrower common law definition been utilised.

Consequently, the significance of the integration, control and economic reality tests are of less importance when interpreting recent statutory regulations, in defining whether a worker has the benefit of the same.

In Byrne Brothers (Sormwork) Ltd v Baird 2002 ICR 667, the EAT had to decide on the status of self employed building trade workers, and whether they were entitled to be accorded the status of a 'worker' pursuant to the Working Time Regulations. The EAT held that these workers were entitled to protection under the Regulations and that for the purposes of defining a 'worker', the existing common law tests would be utilised, albeit with a different cut off point.

It is arguable that a more purposeful result would be achieved if the courts rely less on the traditional common law approaches in defining the employment relationship. Instead, the tribunal and courts should focus more on what goals were intended to be achieved by statutory and regulatory standards, and utilised the concepts of dependency and democratic deficits in determining who should be entitled to benefit from that same.

Chapter 2 – Mutual trust and confidence

In recent years the doctrine of mutual trust and confidence has played an important part in the relationship between employer and employee. It is a common law concept, and assists in the interpretation and performance of certain terms that lie at the heart of the employment relationship.

UK law has traditionally focused on the relationship between employer and employee. As a result, the majority of employment rights apply to employees only. Consequently, workers who work under a contract of services have enjoyed the benefit of these rights, and those workers who perform a contract for services have been excluded.

In recent years there has been a changing view of the employment relationship from that of a purely commercial arrangement between "master" and "servant", towards a more personal relationship. The characteristics of "dependency" and "democratic deficits" should be identified.

It is arguable that dependency and democratic deficits are common to all employment relationships. 'Dependency' means that the employee is reliant upon his employer for work, and 'democratic deficits' implies subordination on the part of the employee to his employer. An 'employee' is identified by the presence of both characteristics, whereas a 'worker' can be dependent on his employer, even where no democratic deficits exist.

It is submitted that the increase in statutory employment regulation, and the growth of common law intervention into the employment relationship, are an indication of the move away from the employment relationship existing on a purely commercial basis.

The employment contract itself is the overriding factor which governs the relationship between the parties. Its express terms determine how the contract is to be performed, and the manner in which the employment is to end. To that extent, the contract should offer certainty to both employer and employee.

However, the courts have recognized that the contract should not be regarded as the only factor in determining the nature and regulation of the employment relationship. Such relationship is something more than a purely commercial arrangement. It is not uncommon for there to have been an inequality of bargaining power between employee and employer at the commencement of employment, and this goes someway to reinforcing the concept of "dependency and democratic deficits".

Consequently, it is submitted that it cannot be right to allow an employer the right to unrestricted enforcement of every term in the employment contract, no matter how unreasonable or oppressive. Similarly, where the contract is silent on a particular issue, it would be unfair to automatically construe in every case such absence against the interests of the employee. There is an argument in favour of common law intervention, and this has been evidenced by the development of implied contractual terms. One of the more important implied terms is that of mutual trust and confidence.

The effect of this implied term is an obligation on the part of the employer that he will treat his employee in a reasonable manner as part of the duty to preserve the relationship of mutual trust and confidence. This means that the employer will not, without reasonable and proper cause, conduct himself in a manner calculated or likely to destroy or seriously damage the relationship of trust and confidence which should exist between him and the employee.

The leading case is Malik v Bank of Credit & Commerce (1997) ICR 606. Here, the employer bank went into liquidation after having operated for sometime in a corrupt and dishonest manner. The court held that this conduct amounted to a breach of the implied contractual obligation of mutual trust and confidence, as the employees employment prospects were tainted by the employers reputation. The House of Lords held that there was a duty on the part of the employer to conduct its business in such a manner so as not to damage its employee's future prospects in the labour market.

In the above case, Lord Nicholls stated, "Employers must take care not to damage their employees' future employment prospects by harsh and oppressive behaviour or by any other form of conduct which is unacceptable today as falling below the standards set by the implied trust and confidence term".

The Malik Case was a culmination of several prior strands running through common law leading up to this House of Lords decision. On earlier occasions, the courts had established that although there was no duty on the employer to act reasonably, the employer was not entitled to behave in an entirely unreasonable manner.

In Isle of White Tourist Board v Coombes 1976 IRLR 413, the employer used foul and abusive language to his personal secretary. The EAT held that this behaviour was totally unacceptable and damaged the confidence which should have existed between the parties. Consequently, the employee was entitled to argue that she had been constructively dismissed.

Similarly, in United Bank v Akhtar 1989 IRLR 1989, the employee claimed constructive dismissal when he had been asked to relocate at very short notice and without financial assistance. His employment contract contained an express clause which stated that he might be required to relocate within the UK on a temporary or permanent basis. The EAT took the view that the lack of reasonable notice and of financial assistance made it impossible for the employee to comply with the contractual obligation to move. The EAT found that the employer's behaviour was intolerable and as such damaged mutual trust and confidence.

It is of crucial importance to note that in the United Bank Case, the EAT did not imply a new or "fair" mobility clause into the employment contract. What was at issue was whether the employer had exercised the existing express mobility clause in a fair and proper manner, and whether the employer's manner of exercising the existing mobility clause was carried out in such a way as to breach mutual trust and confidence.

Is the implied duty on the part of the employer a positive or negative duty? In other words does mutual trust and confidence imply some positive action on the part of the employer to act reasonably, or alternatively, prevent the employer from acting unreasonably in certain circumstances.

In Waltons & Morse v Dorrington 1977 IRLR 488 the applicant non-smoker left her employment in protest at her employer's failure to deal with her complaints about being exposed to cigarette smoke of her fellow employees. The EAT held that there was an implied term on the part of her employer to provide a safe and smoke free environment which was reasonably suitable for the performance of her contractual duties.

In TSB Bank v Harris (2000) IRLR 157, the employer provided a misleading and potentially destructive reference to a potential employer. The EAT held that the employer had failed to act reasonably when compiling the reference, and that this amounted to a breach of mutual trust and confidence.

It is noted that in all the above decisions there had been a "failure" on the part of the employer to act reasonably on the basis of an existing set of circumstances. In the Waltons Case, the employer had failed to reasonably respond to the employees' complaint about her smoke environment. In the TSB Bank Case, the employer had already drafted the reference letter, but had failed to compose it in a reasonable and accurate manner.

Consequently, it is submitted that the implied duty is of a negative nature and arises in response to a situation where the employer has already undertaken an action, and exercised it in an unreasonable manner.

Nevertheless, there are circumstances where trust and confidence will impose a positive obligation on the part of the employer to either carry out or perform a certain act and/or duty. An example of this relates to a female employee's right to return from ordinary or additional maternity leave (Reg 18(1) Maternity & Parental Leave Regulations 1999). In the event of the employee failing to return, it is not sufficient for the employer to assume that the employment relationship has come to an end and treat the contract as discharged. There could be perfectly valid reasons why such an employee has failed to return on the designated date, such as childbirth complications or postnatal depression. Consequently, a prudent employer should carry out reasonable enquiry as to why there has been a failure to return, and failure to do so, may constitute a breach of trust and confidence.

In Visa International Service Association v Paul (2004) IRLR 42, the employee commenced her maternity leave. Shortly after this, here employer decided to reorganise her former department. As part of the reorganisation, her employer created two new posts, and failed to inform the employee of this fact. On her return she was informed that one of the new posts had been filled. The EAT held that the employer was under a duty to keep their employee informed of developments and opportunities, during her period of maternity absence. Failure to do so was a fundamental breach of the implied term of mutual trust and confidence.

Sexual relations with colleagues at work can have significant consequences for both employers and employees. It is arguable that the complexity of sexual relationships which can arise in the workplace is inherently a dangerous combination. The employer should ideally have some policy in place to deal with this situation, particularly if one of the parties is in a vulnerable position. Indeed, some organisations now have policies requiring employees to declare any 'social' relationships with their colleagues. It is often the case that a sexual relationship in the workplace, which becomes a subject matter of an employment dispute, will involve not only breach of trust and confidence, but also an issue of sexual discrimination.

In Reed v Stedman 1999 IRLR 299 the EAT held that the employer's failure to investigate the employee's complaint of sexual harassment, constituted a breach of trust and confidence.

Similarly, in Whitehead v Brighton Marine Palace & Pier Co. Ltd (2005) ET 18/04/05 the employee learned that his manager had used a derogatory homosexual remark about him in his absence. The employee believed that his manager's remark had been influenced by homophobia. The ET found that the employer's remark was offensive and in breach of trust and confidence, as well as amounting to harassment on the grounds of sexual orientation.

Consequently, it is submitted that there is not necessarily an obligation on the part of the employer to prevent sexual harassment in the workplace. The effect of the implied term, is that once sexual harassment has been brought to the employers attention, he should undertake reasonable steps by way of enquiry or investigation to see how the situation can be remedied. A failure to support a victim in the workplace, may constitute a breach. This principle would also apply to an employee who has become the victim of harassment.

In Wigan Borough Council v Davies (1981) ICR 411, the employee was a care assistant. She was 'sent to Coventry' by her fellow care assistants, and there was a refusal by them to cooperate with her at work. Her employers failed to take any significant steps to rectify the situation, and the employee resigned claiming constructive dismissal. The EAT held that the employer was in breach both of the express term to provide reasonable support, and also of an implied contractual term to the same effect.

Trust and confidence is an implied term imposing a duty on the part of the employer not to act in a capricious and subjective manner. However, the employment contract is still of primary importance, and trust and confidence cannot be used to strike out an express contractual clause on the grounds of unreasonability. Priority will be given to the contractual term. When trust and confidence is of particular importance, is where the contract gives some form of discretion on the part of the employer, or where the contract permits variation. In such circumstances, there is an issue as to whether trust and confidence imposes a duty on the employer to exercise such discretion in a reasonable manner.

In White v Reflecting Road Studs Ltd (1991) IRLR 331, the employee transferred from one department to another. The employee's performance in the new department deteriorated. The employment contract contained a cause entitling transfer to an alternative department. The EAT held that it was not correct to assert that the transfer clause had to be exercised in a reasonable manner. Instead, it held that the obligation on the part of the employer was not to act in such a way as to prevent the employee from carrying out his side of the contract.

Conversely, in BPCC Purnell Ltd v Web (1992) EAT/129/90, the employee was also transferred from one department of a company to another. His contract contained a clause requiring 'total flexibility between all departments'. However, upon being transferred to another department, the employee suffered an £80 reduction in weekly salary. This was held to be a clear breach of mutual trust and confidence, as the employer's exercise of the contractual term, with the result in reduction in salary, had substantially altered the basis of the employment relationship.

The boundaries of mutual trust and confidence were further explored in Thornley v Land Securities Trillium Ltd (2005) AELR 194. The employee was employed as an architect. The employer proposed a restructuring which would have the effect of changing the employee's role to that of a managerial position. The EAT held that the proposed change of duties would undermine trust and confidence to the extent that the employee would become de-skilled as an architect.

From the above cases, it can be seen that trust and confidence does not automatically imply a requirement of reasonability on the part of the employer. The fact that the employee works for the worst employer in the land, does not, in itself matter in law. However, there is a requirement that the employer cannot act in an unreasonable manner which is likely to destroy the relationship of trust and confidence between the parties. Thus the issue of reasonability relates to the operation of the employment relationship, and not to the individual employee's needs.

It should always be remembered that employment law is a species of substantive contract law. A contract for the provision of a service is a contract which contains the same fundamental elements as other types of common law contracts, in particular an offer, acceptance, consideration and intention to create legal relations. However, the terms of a provision of a service contract differ from other types of contract, in that its express terms usually dictate the type and manner of the service being provided. In addition and in certain circumstances, statute can imply additional terms into the contract which affect the manner of its performance.

In order for a valid contract to come into existence, there must be an offer from the offeror to the offeree. In Partridge v Crittenden (1968) 2 All ER 421 it was held that an offer should be distinguished from an "invitation to treat". In Carlill v Carbolic Smoke Ball Co (1893) 1 QB 256 it was held that an offer can be made to the whole world. Acceptance of the offer is usually only complete when the offeree's acceptance is received by the offeror. Both parties to the contract must give some benefit to each other, and this is known as consideration. The consideration of one party is given for the consideration of the other and it can either be executed consideration, or executory consideration which is a promise to do something in the future. Past consideration is generally regarded as bad consideration.

The parties to a contract must intend to create a legally binding agreement. Where an agreement is made in a social or domestic context, there is a presumption that the parties did not intend to make a contract, unless there is evidence to the contrary. Conversely, where an agreement is made in a business context, there is a presumption that the parties did intend to make a contract.

A contract which does not contain the essential requirements for its formation will be void. Void contracts are not contracts at all – they have never amounted to a contract and they never will. A contract can be void because of a lack of formalities, or because as in Pearce v Brookes (1866) 1 Exch 213, the contract was illegal. Alternatively, voidable contracts are valid but defective in some way. The contract may operate in every respect as a valid contract until the injured party takes steps to avoid it – In this situation the injured party is given the option to rescind the contract or affirm it and carry on as normal – This right to rescind the contract is known as the equitable remedy of rescission.

In Nash v Inman (1908) 2 KB 1 it was held that only contracts to purchase necessaries are capable of binding a minor. Otherwise they are voidable, or in some cases unenforceable. In Proform Sports Management Ltd v Pro-Active Sports Management Ltd ((2006) EWHC 812 a minor entered into a representation agreement giving a football agent the right to represent him on any transfer negotiations. The contract was held to be voidable and the minor was entitled to avoid it accordingly.

There are also several other situations in which a contract for the provision of a service is voidable, thereby giving the innocent party the remedy of rescission. These include contracts entered into as a result of a mistake, duress, undue influence and misrepresentation.

In Smith v Land & House Property Corporation (1884) 28 ChD 7 a misrepresentation was defined as a false statement of fact inducing an innocent party into a contract. An example of a misrepresentation in the context of a provision of a service, would be a building firm misrepresenting its size and resources in order to secure a large building contract. Under the Misrepresentation Act 1967, the resulting contract is voidable and the appropriate remedy is rescission, (or damages in lieu of rescission).

Every contract contains a set of terms, which are essentially all of the promises which the contract contains. A breach of these terms will provide the innocent party with the remedy for a breach of contract. The express terms of a contract for the provision of a service, will normally depend on the type of service being provided and what the parties actually agreed at the inception of the contract.

The express terms of a contract will be agreed by the parties. In a simple contract for the provision of a service, the usual terms will be what type of service is being provided, the manner and time for performance and the price. Terms are traditionally classified as being either conditions or warranties. In Poussard v Spiers (1876) 1 QBD 410 it was held that a condition is a term which goes to the root of the contract, the breach of which entitles the injured party to terminate the contract and claim damages. On the other

Where an employer seeks to vary an existing contract of employment, then unilateral variation will only be permitted in circumstances where there is express provision in the contract. Alternatively, a contract can be varied by mutual consent but only when both parties agree. In circumstances where the contract permits variation, then mutual trust and confidence is relevant to the manner of variation.

In Kerry Foods Ltd v Lynch (2005) IRLR 680, the employer sought to terminate his employees' contract and re-engage on a new contract incorporating a longer week. The EAT allowed the employers appeal on the basis that the employers service of a lawful notice of termination coupled with an offer of continuous employment on different terms could not in itself amount to a breach of contract.

Thus, if an employer seeks to change the rate of pay, or the place of work, the employee is not bound in law to accept such an alteration unless the instruction is lawful; ie, contractually justified. If not, the only option available to the employer would be to terminate the contract and offer immediate reengagement on modified terms. This may bring clarity to the situation, but at the cost of a possible wrongful and unfair dismissal claim, if the employer is not able to justify 'some other substantial reason'.

The employer is under a duty to maintain trust and confidence throughout the employment relationship and this extends to the work place environment, and protecting the employee from a foreseeable risk of harm.

In the case of Croft v Broadstairs & St Peter's Town Council (2003) EWCA CIV676 the employee had a history of psychiatric illness and suffered a nervous breakdown whilst off work with bronchitis. The employers then commenced a disciplinary procedure, which had the effect of exacerbating her psychiatric condition. The Court held that the employers should have taken into account the employee's psychiatric vulnerability, and that their failure to take this into account when commencing disciplinary procedure was a breach of mutual trust and confidence.

Similarly, in the case of Barber v Somerset County Council (2004) IRLR 475, the employee's teaching post was abolished in a restructuring, and he was given a new post. The employee began to suffer from stress as a result of his new position. The House of Lords held that there was a duty on the part of the employers to take into account the safety of its workers in the light of what it knew or ought to have known about their working conditions. The employer owed a duty of care, and in breach of that duty, the employee suffered a nervous breakdown.

It is arguable that where life has been made intolerable for employees as a result of an inappropriate work place or workload, there could well be an overlap of several implied terms in addition to mutual trust and confidence, such as the employers implied obligation of reasonable care. Indeed, there are situations where the employer could also be in breach of statutory health and safety provisions. Nevertheless, it is also arguable that mutual trust and confidence is a contractual obligation and if viewed in isolation a pure workload complaint should not be brought within its ambit. This appears to suggest that the decided 'work place' and 'workload' cases involve an inappropriate overlap of implied terms and that there needs to be a coherent and consistent application of what relevant implied terms require to be addressed.

We have previously seen how the doctrine of mutual trust and confidence applies during the currency of the contract of employment. What of the dismissal process? In this regard, the issue is to what extent the implied contractual term of trust and confidence can regulate employers' conduct alongside the statutory rights of unfair dismissal.

Employees are at their most vulnerable and in need of protection when faced with dismissal. Their statutory right not to be unfairly dismissed in enshrined in the Employment Rights Act 1996. This stipulates that the employer can only dismiss fairly for one of five statutory dismissal reasons, and provides that the employer must act reasonably in treating them as sufficient for dismissal. In addition, there is now a defined statutory disciplinary and grievance procedure governing the dismissal process.

However, Statute does not provide the employee with any redress for the dismissal process itself other than a compensatory award in the event of an unfair dismissal being established. Hence "stigma" damages are not given statutory recognition, and neither are any psychiactric injuries arising as a result of the employers' behaviour during events leading up to the dismissal.

For many years, the leading authority on this point was Addis v Gramophone Co. Ltd (1909) AC 488. The employees contract entitled him to six months notice of dismissal. The employee was summarily dismissed. The House of Lords were not prepared to uphold the employee's claim for compensation beyond his contractual notice period.

As previously indicated, in the Malik Case the House of Lords had the opportunity of clarifying and giving recognition to the doctrine of mutual trust and confidence. At the same time, their Lordships also revisited the issue of stigma damages. As a result of their employer's fraudulent behaviour, their Lordships concluded that the employees reputation had been harmed in such a way as to limit opportunities for alternative employment. As the breach of trust and confidence had occurred during the currency of their contracts of employment, the employees were entitled to stigma damages accordingly.

The above case appeared to give an opportunity for the common law to recognize a right to damages on the part of an employee who has suffered psychiatric illness as a result of his employer's conduct leading up to the dismissal. The argument is, that the employee's psychiatric injury has arisen as a direct result of his employer's behaviour, and consequently in breach of the implied term of trust and confidence

In Gogay v Hertfordshire County Council (2000) IRLR 703 a residential care worker was suspended for a period of six weeks. As a result she claimed loss of earnings and damages for psychiatric injury. The Court of Appeal held that the employer's behaviour resulted in a breach of mutual trust and confidence, and consequently, the employee's claim for psychiatric loss succeeded.

In the case of Johnson v Unisys Ltd (2001) IRLR 279 the employee claimed that his dismissal was unfair because proper procedures were not followed. Consequently, he asserted that there had been a breach of mutual trust and confidence by virtue of the manner of his dismissal, and that he should be entitled to stigma damages. The House of Lords disagreed. The court held by a majority that it would not be correct to extend the statutory provisions for unfair dismissal into the common law. The court reiterated that the doctrine of trust and confidence could only apply during the currency of the employment contract, and not afterwards, during the notice period, when the contract had come to an end.

The above case appears to establish what is known as the "Johnson exclusion zone". Effectively, a claim for psychiatric loss arising out of the dismissal is excluded, whilst pre-dismissal psychiatric injury is not. Therefore, it appears that in this area, the obligation of mutual trust and confidence on the part of the employer has more limited application.

The above issue was again revised by the House of Lords in Eastwood v Magnox Plc (2005) AC 503. In this case, the applicant suffered psychiatric injury as a result of a malicious pre-dismissal disciplinary procedure. The employers conduct was undoubtedly a breach of trust and confidence. On a strict interpretation of the Johnson case ante, the applicant would not be entitled to damages as the employers malicious behavior related to the manner of dismissal. However, the House of Lords drew a line between a pre-dismissal behaviour as opposed to the employers' behaviour on dismissal. The employer would be fixed with liability relating to behaviour occurring prior to the date of dismissal, and consequently Mr Eastwood was entitled to recover damages accordingly.

Nevertheless, the House of Lords reiterated that the Johnson case remained good law and that an employee would not be entitled to damages relating to his employers behaviour in connection with dismissal itself. In the judgment, Lord Nichols expressed the hope that parliament would legislate to extend the doctrine of mutual trust and confidence at common law to the manner of the actual dismissal process itself.

In Sutherland v Hatton 2002 IRLR 263, the Court of Appeal set out specified requirements in order for an employee to successfully establish work related psychiatric stress. These were entitled "sixteen practical propositions", and were broadly similar to existing requirements in the tort of negligence. Consequently, there was a requirement for the employee to establish a duty of care, breach of duty, reasonable foreseeability and damage. Barrett felt that as a result of this case, it is difficult for an employee to successfully establish a stress claim based on negligence. Particular difficulty is had with regard to establishing reasonable forseeability on the part of the employer.

There could be a distinction between stress related claims being presented in tort and such claims being litigated in contract. In the former case, a stress related claim must show all the required elements of negligence in order to succeed. However a stress related claim presented in breach of the employment contract has the advantage of being able to be based on a breach of the implied term of mutual trust and confidence.

It is arguable that the limitations on presenting a stress related workplace claim in tort are such, that any expansion in this area of law is likely to be more successful if based on mutual trust and confidence. Nevertheless, there are still significant limitations on a stress related mutual trust and confidence claim, such as the previously mentioned "Johnson Zone". Until the post dismissal Johnson Zone is judicially dealt with, employers can escape liability for the continuing effects of stress by terminating the employment.

The relationship between employer and employee is founded on a continuing bond of trust and confidence, which is represented in the implied term. However, the employment relationship is a two way process, and there is also an obligation on the part of the employee not to destroy the bond of trust and confidence. Such obligation on the part of the employee is manifested in the common law duty of fidelity. The employee's duty of fidelity is implied into every contract of employment, and includes non-competition, a duty of honesty and accounting for profits. An employee's breach of the duty of fidelity can amount to misconduct.

In Neary v Dean of Westminster (1999) IRLR 288 the employee was an organist at Westminster Abbey. He used his position as organist to enter into recording contrcts for his own benefit. The employee's failure to disclose to his employer the profits which had been made from these recording contacts, was held to be a breach of the duty of fidelity.

A similar breach of fidelity occurred in Hivac Ltd v Park Royal Scientific Instruments Ltd 1946 Ch 169, where the highly skilled employees were held to be in breach of their duty of fidelity when manufacturing in their spare time the same type of instruments which were being made for their employer.

The age of the Hivac case is interesting, on the basis that the employee's duty of fidelity pre-dates the more modern principle of trust and confidence.At that time, the common law was more inclined to enforce the duties of an employee, rather than than any obligation on the part of his employer.

There consequently appears to be two distinct implied common law duties, namely that of mutual trust and confidence and the employers implied duty to exercise reasonable care. The latter duty, is a more traditional implied duty and incorporates an obligation to take reasonable care for the employees welfare, health and safety. It is questionable whether these two distinct duties have overlapped to the extent that there is now a single all embracing over-arching principle, to which all other implied duties on the part of the employer are subject.

In Johnstone v Bloomsbury Health Authority 1992 QB333, the Court of Appeal held that where the contract contained an express term which conflicted with the implied term of trust and confidence, then the implied term would prevail. In short, any express contractual term must coexist with mutual trust and confidence, in order to remain valid.

Similarly, any express contractual term which provides the employer with a discretionary power, must also be read in conjunction with the implied term, in terms of exercising that discretion.

In Imperial Group Pension Trust Ltd v Imperial Tobacco Ltd & Harkulak (1991) IRLR 66, there was an occupational pension scheme in place. Under the terms of this Scheme, the employer had the power to refuse consent to increases of pension benefits. The court held that the employer had to exercise this power in accordance with the implied obligation of trust and confidence.

The analysis of judicial decisions incorporating mutual trust and confidence, is in his opinion, an interpretation of the employers duty of good faith, rather than constraints on the employers exercise of discretionary power. Therefore, it is arguable that this mitigates against mutual trust and confidence developing into an over-arching principle incorporating a duty to exercise reasonable care.

In conclusion, the implied duties on the part of the employer remain distinct, and that there is no evidence for the emergence of mutual trust and confidence becoming an over-arching principle incorporating other established implied duties. The concept of trust and confidence developing into an over-arching principle remains an unfulfilled common law aspiration.

What then can be concluded about the present development of trust and confidence? There is no doubt that the implied term has been of help to employees in recent years. It has prevented employers from acting in an arbitrary and capricious manner, especially where an express contractual clause confers some element of discretion on the part of the employer.

It is submitted that the present effect of trust and confidence is to introduce into the arena of employment law a set of principles, very much akin to equitable principles, running concurrently with the common law.

However, and as previously mentioned, trust and confidence does not impose a general duty of reasonability on the part of the employer. Neither does the implied term automatically strike-out an express term. Consequently, it is not accepted that employers are now prevented from understanding which term in the contract they are entitled to enforce. An employer is still entitled to refer to the contact and enforce a contractual term, so long as he does not act in a manner likely to breach trust and confidence.

Chapter 3 – The European perspective (TUPE)

A transfer of ownership or merger of a business invariably has consequences for its employees and their contracts of employment. The right of an employee to employment protection in the event of a transfer or merger of an undertaking, was initially protected by the Acquired Rights Directive 1977.

The latest Acquired Rights Directive updates such protection, and operates as a consolidation directive. It is associated with the Collective Redundancy Directive and the Protection from Insolvency Directive.

All three Directives have their origins in the Social Action Programme 1974 which envisaged the development of the internal market and economic harmonisation within the Community. The Programme foresaw that there would be significant economic change within the Community. As a consequence the aim of the three Directives was to assist in the management of change insofar as protecting employment rights was concerned.

In the UK, implementation of the AR Directive 1977 was effected by the Transfer of Undertakings (Protection of Employment) Regulations 1981. Since April 2006, these Regulations have now been superseded by the Transfer of Undertakings (Protection of Employment) Regulations 2006. The issue arises as to what extent TUPE 2006 has adequately implemented the AR Directive.

Before discussing whether the present UK response to the AR Directive has been adequately effected, it is necessary to examine the method by which European law is implemented into the legislative process of member states.

There are three types of European legislation, namely Treaty articles, regulations and directives. The European Parliament together with the Council and the Commission can make regulations and issue directives. Some articles are "directly applicable" and can have both "vertical direct effect" and "horizontal direct effect". Vertical direct effect means that EU legislation can be enforced by an individual against the state or emanation of the state. Horizontal direct effect means that they can be used in claims brought by individual citizens against another individual of the member state.

In Van Gend en Loos the ECJ held that Treaty provisions were capable of conferring directly effective rights on individuals. However, the principle of direct effect would only apply to those provisions which were sufficiently "precise and unconditional".

Unlike some of the Treaty articles, a directive will not be directly applicable. It requires each member state to incorporate the directive in order to be given effect in the national legal system. In the UK, this requires an Act of Parliament or delegated legislation. The directive will set out the results to be achieved, but will leave some choice to each member state as to its precise form and implementation.

Transposition of the AR Directive into the UK in the form of TUPE 2006, has been effected by virtue of powers contained in Section 2(2) of the European Communities Act 1972 and Section 38 Employment Relations Act 1999.

There is a general rule, that when implementing a directive, a member state should not exceed the ambit of the originating directive. Hence, the significance of invoking Section 38 ERA 1999, was to enable the UK to effect implementation of TUPE 2006 in excess of the AR Directive's provisions.

An unimplemented directive is capable of having vertical direct effect. It is not capable of having horizontal direct effect. In Ratti, the ECJ held that an unimplemented directive can only be enforced by an individual against the recalcitrant member state, once the deadline for implementation of the directive has passed.

Where a directive has vertical direct effect, an individual employed by the state, or "emanation" of it, can claim against his employer the rights given by the directive. Unfortunately, a worker who is not employed by an "emanation of the state" cannot claim under the directive in this situation.

In Foster v British Gas the ECJ held that the Equal Treatment Directive could be used by individuals employed by anybody made responsible by the state for providing a public service under its control.

Article 1 of the AR Directive 1977, provided that it would apply to an "undertaking, business or part of a business". This was implemented into Regulation 2(1) of TUPE 1981 as applying to an "undertaking" which would include any trade or business, but not including any undertaking which wasn't in the nature of a commercial venture.

Consequently, in Woodcock v Friends School Wigton the CA held that several teachers were unable to claim the protection of TUPE 1981 against unfair dismissal, because the school was a charitable body.

Conversely, in Dr Sophie Redmond Stichting the ECJ held differently and decided that the AR Directive 1977 would protect employees of a drug rehabilitation foundation who lost their jobs when local authority funding was withdrawn.

The AR Directive 1977 was subsequently amended in an attempt to resolve judicial uncertainty by Directive 98/50/EC. Wholesale consolidation was eventually effected by the AR Directive.

For the AR Directive to apply, the undertaking must be transferred in a recognisable form from one employer to another. This previously created difficulties in circumstances where there had been a service provision changes. Such term applies when an employer engages a contractor to perform service activities and those activities are accordingly contracted out, or, the service contract ends and is assigned to a different contractor or alternatively is brought back in-house.

In the case of Spijkers the ECJ held that in determining whether a "transfer of an undertaking" has taken place, the overall test was whether the business in question had retained its identity, this being indicated in particular by the continuation or resumption of its operation by the new employer.

Consequently, in Schmidt the Claimant was a cleaner at a bank. Her employer contracted out her cleaning duties to another company resulting in her being offered a job with the new contactor for less pay. In applying the Spijkers test, the ECJ held that despite there being no transfer of assets, a stable economic entity had transferred which had retained its identity after the transfer.

However, in the later case of Suzen , the ECJ appeared to depart from Spijkers and Schmidt. Here, the Claimant was dismissed by a school cleaning contractor after the cleaning contract was relocated from another contractor. The ECJ drew a distinction between an "economic entity" and an "activity". The entity was more than the activity, and consequently a mere transfer of the activity was not enough to fall within the ambit of the directive. There had to be a transfer of an entity, and this would be difficult to prove where neither significant assets nor a major part of the workforce had been transferred.

The Suzen Case attracted judicial criticism as it provided a mechanism to by-pass TUPE 1981, by ensuring that the transferee contractor took over none of the transferor's employers.

In ECM Ltd v Cox, the Court of Appeal attempted to reconcile the apparent conflict between Schmidt and Suzen. The CA looked at the motive behind the transfer, and decided that if it was obvious that an attempt was being made to avoid the consequences of a transfer, then the transferee should not be entitled to rely on Suzen purely for such purpose.

Similarly in Francisco Hernandez Vidal , the ECJ held that both a relocation of a contract and the resumption of a subcontracted cleaning activity by the main undertaking fell within the AR Directive.

The Preamble to the present AR Directive is most illuminating, and to a certain extent attempts to clarify the reasons behind its introduction.

Clauses 3 and 4 of the Preamble, recognise the necessity in protecting the interests of employees in the event of a change of employer. The fact that there remained differences between member states as to the extent of protection, was recognised, and the objective of reducing such differences was stated.

Clauses 5 and 7 recognised that the establishment of the internal market established a need for greater harmonisation and improvement of living and working conditions for workers within the EU. Clause 8 reiterated that terminology in respect of the definition of a "transfer" for the purposes of the Directive, required to be brought up to date in light of previous decisions of the ECJ.

Consequently it is submitted that the AR Directive attempted to clarify the scope of the earlier AR Directive 1977, in the light of subsequent case law of the ECJ, relating in particular to the safeguarding of employees' rights on a transfer, and the "contracting out of services" by the employer.

Article 1(b) of the AR Directive 2001 states that a transfer has taken place when "there is a transfer of an economic entity which retains its identity, meaning an organised grouping of resources which has the objective of pursuing an economic activity, whether or not that activity is central or ancillary".

Article 2(d) of the AR Directive 2001 also defines an employee to be "any person who, in the member state concerned, is protected as an employee under National employment law'.

Upon clarification of the definition of what constitutes an appropriate transfer, and definition of the parties, Articles 3 and 4 specify the nature of protected rights. The Articles provide that employee rights are to be protected in the event of the merger or acquisition of an economic entity, or part of an economic entity. Such transfer cannot in itself result in the dismissal of employees and the transferee must assume the rights and obligations in all contracts of employment.

The original AR Directive 1977 was silent as to transfers arising as a result of corporate insolvency. This was a major defect as many transfers occur as a result of corporate distress, and in this regard the Directive failed to address the "management of change", which was the aim of the 1974 Social Action Programme.

Consequently, Article 5 provides that where the transferor is the subject of bankruptcy or insolvency proceedings, Member States would be entitled to make provision to safeguard the interests of employees on a transfer. This could include a variation of terms and conditions of employment, if such variation were to result in the survival of the business.

The AR Directive also requires that any Collective agreements must be honoured until they expire or are replaced by another agreement. Article 7 imposes an obligation on the transferor and transferee to inform the employees' representatives "in good time" prior to the transfer of the reasons for such transfer, and the legal, economic, and social implications of the transfer.

Review of the history of the AR Directive, and also the development of the ECJ's interpretation of "transfer of undertaking", suggests that the ECJ has attempted to strike a suitable balance between the need to protect employees' rights on a transfer and the need to ensure the competitiveness and economic efficiency of undertakings.

The Oy Liikenne case is also relevant. Here a bus company transferred its bus routes and bus drivers. The bus company retained its buses. The ECJ held that there was a transfer of employees, but not of assets in an undertaking based significantly on tangible assets. Consequently the transfer of the workforce alone did not trigger an application of the AR Directive. The issue of whether an undertaking had retained its identity or whether there had been a transfer of assets and/or workforce, would depend on the facts of each case which in turn would be down to a National court to interpret. The AR Directive does not achieve full harmonisation in this area, and give a significant degree of flexibility in application, to individual Member states.

Within the past ten years, the public sector has undergone considerable change with regard to the operation and delivery of services. One of the reasons underpinning such change is the introduction of the Public Private Partnership as an initiative involving the private sector in the operation of public services. This includes "contracting out", privatisation and the development of the Private Finance Initiative.

The above developments invariably result in a transfer of employees. Such transfer will either be within the public sector, or, from the public to the private sector. In each situation, the issue arises as to whether a relevant transfer has taken place for the purposes of the AR Directive and/or TUPE Regulations

In Henke , the ECJ held that the transfer of administrative functions from one local authority to a new larger authority, would not be covered by the AR Directive 1977. In this case, a German municipality was merged with other councils to form a larger administrative unit. The ECJ was of the opinion that this was a reorganisation of structure of a public administration, and consequently fell outside the Directive.

As previously discussed, the mere transfer of assets did not fall within the scope of TUPE 1981. The combined effect of Spijkers and Suzen was that in order to determine whether a protected transfer had taken place, the overall test was whether an identifiable economic entity has been transferred, and, whether such entity had continued after transfer in an identifiable form.

Under pressure from the Trade Union movement, the Government attempted to address public sector contracting exercises involving staff transfers. Consequently, in 2000 the Cabinet Office issued a Statement of Practice on Staff Transfers in the Public Sector ('COS 2000').

Clause 6 COS, establishes a framework to be followed by public sector organisations in order to give effect to Government policy on the treatment of staff transfers, where the public sector is the employer in contracting situations, or the client in a re-tendering situation

Where there is a transfer as a result of a Public Private Partnership, Clause 11 COS recognises that the application of TUPE will be a matter of law based on the individual facts of the particular transfer. Consequently, the issue of whether an economic entity has been transferred and continues in an identifiable form remains relevant.

However, Clause 11 COS goes onto to state that the public sector contracting authority should endeavour to ensure when inviting tenders, that potential bidders submit their proposal on the basis that the TUPE Regulations will apply to employees affected by such transfer. It is submitted that this creates a "level playing field" for all potential bidders.

With regard to a transfer within the public sector, Clause 18 COS recognises that TUPE and/or the AR Directive may not apply in each case on the basis of there being a transfer of an administrative function. The Henke judgment is specifically mentioned.

Consequently, Clause 19 COS provides that on a relevant transfer, the transferring public body should ensure that provision is to be made for staff to transfer on TUPE terms, "irrespective of whether the transfer is excluded from the scope of the Directive implemented by TUPE". Government departments should also ensure that the transfer should follow the principles of TUPE, "along with appropriate arrangements to protect occupational pension, redundancy and severance terms'.

It is important to note that COS is a policy statement and is not enforceable per se. Its purpose was to confirm the application of existing TUPE protection into public sector contracting initiatives. Nevertheless, it is questionable as to whether COS is an acceptable mechanism of indirectly imposing an EU directive.

The UK's response to the AR Directive 2001 was effected on 6th April 2006 by virtue of TUPE 2006. The DTI Guidance provides that the aim and effect of TUPE 2006, "is to preserve the continuity of employment and terms and conditions of those employees who are transferred to a new employer when a relevant transfer takes place" .

Regulation 3(1)(a) defines a "relevant transfer" for the purposes of TUPE 2006. It applies to a transfer of an undertaking or part of an undertaking where, "there is a transfer of an economic entity which retains its identity". Regulation 3(2) defines an "economic entity" as an "organised grouping of resources which has the objective of pursuing an economic activity".

It is noted that the above definitions of "transfer" and "economic entity", transpose the definitions of these terms specified in Article 1(b) of the AR Directive 2001.

However, with regard to the definition of a "service provision change", it is submitted that TUPE 2006 goes further than the AR Directive 2001. It has already been seen that the combined effect of Spijkers and Suzen have resulted in uncertainty as to whether TUPE 1981 and the AR Directive sufficiently covered this type of transfer.

Regulation 3(1)(b) TUPE 2006 specifically defines a service provision change, and utilises the word "activities" as a broad term to cover the nature of service provision. Pursuant to Regulation 3(3), three conditions are necessary in order for the Regulations to apply to a service provision change;

1. There must be an organised grouping of employees whose principal purpose is to carry out the relevant activities for the client, and,
2. The client must intend that the activities will be carried out by the transferee after the service provision change, other than in connection with a single event or task, and,
3. The activities are not for the supply of goods.

It is further submitted that TUPE 2006 clarification on service provision changes should result in increased certainty with less scope for litigation. The parties will know where they stand prior to the transfer and apportion risks accordingly. In addition, there is less likelihood of an undertaking being able to unfairly "undercut" another with regard to employee costs, in a competitive tendering situation.

Regulation 4 TUPE 2006 endeavours to transpose Article 4 of the AR Directive. It sets out what happens to a contract of employment on transfer. Existing terms in the contract of employment are to continue in the same way under the transferee employer as they operated under the transfer employer.

Under Regulation 4(2) TUPE 2006 any variation to the employment contract due to the transfer will be void, unless effected for an economic, technical or organisational reason (ETO reason) relating to the transfer. However, it is suggested that the reason why a transferee will seek to vary an employment term is in order to seek harmonisation with existing employees. Nevertheless, such harmonisation will not qualify as an ETO reason.

In accordance with Article 4(2) of the AR Directive 2001, an employee who is dismissed as a result of a transfer, is given protection under Regulation 7 TUPE 2006. This will be regarded as constituting an automatically unfair dismissal. Similarly, Regulation 4(9) TUPE 2006 allows for an employee to claim constructive dismissal in the event of an unwarranted variation of contractual terms.

There is however a caveat to the interpretation of Regulations 4 and 7 TUPE 2006, when dealing with the issue of a dismissal on transfer. As previously indicated, a dismissal is automatically unfair when the employee is dismissed as a result of the transfer. Yet the same dismissal could be potentially fair if it has arisen as a result of a variation dependent upon an ETO. There potentially appears to be two competing principal reasons, with their origins in different parts of the AR Directive.

Article 3(2) of the AR Directive 2001 imposes an obligation of the part of the transferor to notify the transferee of "all rights and obligations" which are subject to the transfer. Consequently, Regulation 11 TUPE 2006 imposes a duty on the part of the transferor to provide written information in advance to the transferee, about the contracts of employment of those employees affected by the transfer.

Failure to provide such "employee liability information" will allow the transferee to present a claim to an employment tribunal and seek an award in respect of each employee in respect of whom information was incorrect. This new obligation is a significant new protection for transferees, and the potential award appears to go further than the protection offered by the AR Directive 2001.

Article 7 of the AR Directive 2001 imposes a duty on the transferor and transferee to inform and consult with representatives of employees affected by the proposed transfer. There was no obligation on the part of either party to furnish this information in TUPE 1981.

The issue of corporate distress is addressed by Regulations 8 and 9, and implement Article 5 of the AR Directive 2001. Pursuant to Regulation 8, any pre-existing liabilities to employees, do not pass to the transferee, insofar as such liabilities are capable of being discharged out of the National Insurance Fund. The aim of this, is to promote corporate rescue by making the undertaking more attractive to a potential purchaser.

Similarly, Regulation 9 provides for a "permitted variation" of terms and conditions on transfer after agreement with employee representatives. However, the reason for the "permitted variation" must be the transfer itself and designed to safeguard employment opportunities. Nevertheless, it is difficult to see how employee representatives can negotiate on an equal basis, if they are negotiating under threat of unemployment.

Regulations 13-15 impose an obligation on both the transferor and transferee to inform and consult with employee representatives about the proposed transfer. A failure to inform and consult will render both parties jointly and severally liable to discharge any Tribunal award connected with such failure. This right to seek an award again appears to go further than the original AR Directive.

It is interesting to note that whereas Article 7(5) of the AR Directive 2001 allows member states to limit the obligation to consult with employee representatives in circumstances where there appears to be a small undertaking, no such "small business exemption", appears in TUPE 2006.

It is noted that the overriding effect of Regulations 11 and 13-15 TUPE 2006 will be that when drafting business transfer agreements, a prudent draftsman will advise each party to seek their own contractual provisions, not least including specific indemnities to clarify who exactly will be responsible for paying any compensation in the event of any breach.

It is submitted that the government has made a reasonable attempt to transpose the provisions of the AR Directive 2006 into TUPE 2006. As has been seen, many TUPE 2006 Regulations clearly emanate from the AR Directive.

An example of effective transposition is that of Regulation 3 TUPE 2006, where the definitions of "transfer" and "economic entity" have been expressly defined so as to address judicial uncertainty and remove anachronistic wording.

The issues surrounding a service provision change have been clarified and it is submitted that a satisfactory attempt has been made in the Regulations to address the uncertainty resulting from Suzen. In this regard, TUPE 2006 appears to have exceeded the ambit of the AR Directive.

Nevertheless, uncertainty as to whether TUPE applies to transfers within the public sector have not been addressed by TUPE 2006. Therefore COS 2000 remains applicable within the Public Sector.

Chapter 4 – The European perspective (ECHR)

The European Convention on Human Rights is one of the earliest and most important treaties passed by the Council of Europe, a group of nations invited by Sir Winston Churchill to come together after the Second World War to stop such atrocities and acts of cruelty happening again. The Council of Europe is quite separate from the EU. It has its own Court of Human Rights in Strasbourg. Until 1998, the ECHR was not been part of the UK's domestic law. However the HRA 1998 effectively incorporated the ECHR into UK law.

Art. 3 ECHR provides that "no one shall be subjected to torture or to inhuman or degrading treatment or punishment." It is a positive right and imposes a duty on the part of the State to protect individuals against a violation of their human right not to suffer the ill-treatment envisaged by the Article.

The traditional UK approach is one of protection of civil liberties. There was no positive duty to prevent ill-treatment, and the common law's negative approach was to allow an individual or the State to undertake an act unless prevented by law.

The UK was one of the original signatories to the 1950 Convention. However, because of the dualist approach taken by the UK in the context of international law, the ECHR was not incorporated into UK law.

Unlike a monist State, such as France, international treaties are not automatically incorporated. The doctrine of Parliamentary supremacy inhibits international obligations overriding primary legislation. Successful incorporation of an international treaty requires the enacting of enabling legislation by Parliament.

Prior to 1998, the ECHR did not form part of UK law, and domestic legislation and jurisprudence had priority. Its status was the same as several other international treaties outlawing torture such as UNCAT and the Universal Declaration of Human Rights. It only had persuasive influence as a judicial aid to interpretation in cases of ambiguity.

Incorporation of the ECHR was finally achieved by virtue of the Human Rights Act 1998 ("the HRA"). Section 3 HRA, provides that all primary and subordinate legislation must be read and given effect in a way that is compatible with the Convention.

The principle purpose of the ECHR is to protect an individual against a violation of their Convention rights by either the State or public authority of the State. This is the "vertical" effect of the Convention, which is principally concerned with protection of the individual's human rights viz a viz the State.

Section 6(1) HRA provides that it is unlawful for a public authority to act in a way which is incompatible with a Convention right. This includes UK courts and tribunals. Under s7 HRA, a victim of an unlawful act can rely on Convention rights to bring proceedings against the public authority in the appropriate court or tribunal, or, rely upon a Convention right in any legal proceedings.

Section 2 HRA provides that in determining any issue arising out of a Convention right, UK courts and tribunals must take into account any judgment of the ECtHR and/or decision of the European Commission for Human Rights, ("the ECmHR"). This has given rise to a "horizontal" effect, in that the courts are obliged to protect individuals against infringement of their Convention rights by other individuals.

As an absolute right, Art. 3 is incapable of derogation. Furthermore, unlike other Articles, there is no limitation or qualification on its effect. A Convention right subject to a qualification, is capable of being defended by virtue of a legitimate aim. However, there is no such defence to a breach of Art. 3, as there are no circumstances in which the state can properly justify the exercise of torture.

In Tomasi v France the ECtHR nade it clear that the use of torture to extract information, even if used to combat terrorism, was unjustifiable. In his article entitled "Torture" Malcolm Evans discusses the ongoing debate as to whether any circumstances exist to justify the exercise of torture in order to prevent harm being caused to others. This is a debate which has increased in intensity since the events of Sept 11th, and the ensuing "war on terror".

Evans noted a balance of competing concerns between those who take the moral "high ground" by asserting that there can never be any circumstances in which a state can have recourse to torture, and those who take a more pragmatic view, such as Alan Dershowitz who has argued in favour of the judiciary issuing "torture warrants". He recognises that the debate is ongoing, and opinions may shift with changing circumstances.

Prior to the HRA, injury arising from torture was already unlawful. However there was no positive right or duty within UK law to prevent ill-treatment. The HRA effectively created a rights based system, centred on the protection of human rights, as opposed to preservation of traditional residual liberties.

There has been a traditional common law aversion against ill-treatment, and the acceptance of evidence obtained under torture as a method of proof. The case of A v Home Secretary is relevant. Here, the Supreme Court was firmly of the view that evidence obtained by torture should be excluded from UK courts, not only on the basis of Convention rights, but also on the basis of traditional common law jurisprudence.

A major impact of incorporation of Art 3 within the UK, is that the Article covers situations which are not necessarily criminal and often have nothing to do with a crime being committed.

In Chahal v United Kingdom" the ECtHR considered the effect that deportation would have on an individual in circumstances where there was a risk of torture at the hands of the receiving government. The potential risk of torture by the receiving Punjabi government constituted a breach of Art. 3, because of the positive obligation within the Article to prevent torture.

The fact that the applicant in Chahal had not lawfully entered the UK, was held not to be important. At the time of the application, the applicant was within the jurisdiction of a Contracting State, and this was sufficient to enable him to rely upon a Convention right. In addition, the ECtHR reiterated in Chahal that the "absolute" nature of Art. 3 meant that the UK was bound to protect an individual within its jurisdiction from torture, even if such ill-treatment was likely to take place outside the UK.

In Chahal, the ECtHR was spared the difficult task of deciding whether or not it had been established that the applicant was a security risk. In view of its absolute nature, this issue was simply irrelevant to the application of Art. 3. Hence although Art. 3 provides a guarantee against ill-treatment, it is not a bar to deportation in general. The applicant in Chahal could still have been deported without violating Art. 3, had he been sent from the UK to a third, more peaceful country. With this in mind, it becomes necessary to carefully examine the potential ill-treatment that the applicant is likely to suffer at the hands of the receiving state.

In Soering v United Kingdom the USA sought extradition from the UK of an individual accused of murder in circumstances where he faced the death penalty. The UK government had already received an undertaking from US prosecutors that the UK's view on the death penalty would be taken into account in the determination of sentence. The ECtHR nonetheless held that the circumstances leading up to the exercise of the death penalty, and in particular, the "death row" phenomenon, constituted a violation of Art. 3.

The Soering principle was affirmed in the later case of HLR v France where the ECtHR held that Art. 3 applied even in circumstances where the deported individual faced a risk of torture from individuals based in the receiving state, which in this case were Columbian drug dealers. The appropriate test was twofold – Firstly whether the deportation would result in a real risk of the individual being subjected to the alleged treatment, and, secondly, whether such treatment would be in violation of Art. 3.

For a breach of Art. 3 to be established in deportation or extradition cases, it must be proved that the victim faces a "clear risk" of ill-treatment in the receiving state. In Vilvarajah v UK the applicants faced deportation from the UK to Sri Lanka, where they claimed that due to the unsettled conditions at that time they would face ill treatment in breach of Art 3. The ECtHR held that the applicants were unable to show a clear risk of ill treatment which would be different from that of existing Sri Lankan residents. The risk of their treatment being in breach of the Convention was a "mere possibility", and this was not sufficient to establish an obligation on the part of the UK.

A review of the use of diplomatic assurances when the UK is faced with the deportation of foreign nationals, is relevant. It is noted that the "quality" of the diplomatic assurance is dependent upon the nature of the state providing the same, and whether such state has a history of condoning the use of torture.

The definition of torture contained in Art. 3 goes beyond the traditional concept of what constitutes torture. It contains three elements, consisting of torture per se, inhuman treatment or punishment, or degrading treatment or punishment. A violation of any of these elements will be in breach of the Article.

In Ireland v United Kingdom the ECtHR had the opportunity of examining "five techniques" utilised by the UK in the detention of suspects in Northern Ireland. These included deprivation of food and sleep, being forced to stand against a wall, hooding and intense noise. The Court held that "torture" constituted deliberate inhuman treatment causing serious and cruel suffering, "inhuman treatment" included the infliction of intense physical and mental suffering and "degrading treatment" included acts designed to cause humiliation, fear debasement and inferiority.

The ECtHR in Ireland found that the application of the five techniques, constituted both inhuman treatment and degrading treatment because they caused intense physical and mental suffering, resulting in fear and humiliation. Nevertheless, the Court also found that the techniques did not amount to torture because they did not amount to deliberate treatment causing serious and cruel suffering. Even so, a breach of Art. 3 had occurred due to the presence of at least two of the requisite elements.

In many situations the presence of torture is self evident, such as in Aydin v Turkey where the victim was raped, blindfolded and beaten. In the Greek Case the ECmHR made a distinction between inhuman treatment which was deliberate and caused serious and cruel suffering, and inhuman treatment which caused mental or physical suffering. The former constituted torture, and the latter inhuman treatment or punishment.

A finding of torture is usually reserved for those acts which result in the most severe forms of inhuman and degrading treatment. The threshold is typically crossed in circumstances where the perpetrator has deliberately set out on a course of inhuman and degrading treatment taking into account the level of harm suffered by the victim.

In Denmark v Greece the ECmHR found that the intensity of mental suffering inflicted on a victim over a period of time resulting in psychological injury was capable of constituting torture. In Selmouni v France torture was held to have taken place after the victim had been urinated upon, subjected to verbal abuse and threatened with a blow torch. In this case, the ECtHR reiterated that the Convention is a "living instrument" which should be interpreted in the light of present day conditions. Therefore, what may have in the past be defined as "inhuman and degrading", might now be regarded as torture.

Inhuman treatment involves a serious attack on a victim's physical mental or psychological well being. Hence application of the five techniques utilised in the Ireland Case constituted both inhuman and degrading treatment. In A v UK the ECtHR held that in order to characterise treatment as inhuman, it must reach a minimum level of severity.

In Tomasi v France the fact that the victim was hit, slapped, kicked and humiliated constituted both inhuman and degrading treatment. The attack on his physical and mental wellbeing was held to be inhuman treatment.

Nevertheless, inhuman treatment can arise in the absence of physical violence as in the case of Dulas v Turkey. Here, the victim was forced to watch security services demolish her house where she had lived all her life. Her vulnerability in the face of armed soldiers destroying her property, was held to constitute inhuman treatment.

The threshold for establishing degrading treatment appears to be lower than that of torture and inhuman treatment. In Delazarous v UK the victim was held in solitary confinement for four months. The ECtHR held that such treatment would be degrading and thus in breach of Art. 3 "if it arouses in the victim a feeling of fear, anguish and inferiority capable of humiliating and possibly breaking his physical or moral resistance".

In reality, the boundary between inhuman treatment and degrading treatment is likely to be more blurred. Hence in Tyrer v UK a juvenile had been sentenced by a court in the Isle of Man to three strokes of the birch. The ECtHR held that the ill treatment suffered by the victim was not sufficient to reach the level of "torture" or "inhuman treatment". Nevertheless, such ill treatment was held to be degrading, as it involved a degree of humiliation or debasement which exceeded that which was usual in punishment.

It should be noted that the ECtHR has not outlawed corporal punishment, as there is no violation of Art. 3 simply in administering a punishment. In Costello-Roberts v UK a seven year old child was punished with application of "the slipper" on his buttocks at a private school. The ECtHR held that the punishment in this case had not produced any severe or long lasting effects. In order to establish a violation of Art. 3, it was necessary to show that the punishment had reached a minimum level of severity, and such threshold had not been achieved in this case.

A similar conclusion had already been reached in the pre-HRA case of Campbell & Cosans v UK where two pupils at a school had been threatened with the use of a cane across the hand. The ECtHR held that threat of use of the cane did not breach Art. 3 as they had not suffered punishment, and neither was there any evidence of humiliation or debasement on the part of either of the boys.

Consequently, it is submitted that the level of punishment and its effect on the victim, is of significant importance in determining whether corporal punishment constitutes inhuman and/or degrading treatment. The place of punishment and by whom it is administered may also be highly significant. Hence in Warwick v UK a sixteen year old female pupil received corporal punishment from a male teacher in front of another male teacher. The Commission found that her punishment had been humiliating and had reached a sufficient level of seriousness to constitute degrading treatment.

In X v UK the fourteen year old victim suffered a caning at school which produced a scar across her buttocks resulting in discomfort for several days. The Commission declared this to be a violation of Art. 3. Similarly, in Y v UK a fifteen year old victim received a caning resulting in bruising and swelling to his buttocks. The Commission again found there to be an admissible claim under Art. 3.

Corporal punishment in schools has now been outlawed by virtue of s131 School Standards and Framework Act 1998. However, the common law recognised the defence of "lawful chastisement", and therefore the issue of punishment within the family environment remained outstanding.

In A v UK the ECtHR held that beatings with a garden cane administered with considerable force to a nine year old boy by his step-father, violated Art. 3. As a result of this case, the extent of lawful chastisement is limited to it not resulting in inhuman or degrading treatment.

As a "living instrument", each Article of the ECHR should not be read in isolation. In many cases, a victim may seek to argue that his treatment has been in violation of one or more Articles of the Convention. Some provisions such as Art. 2 (Right to life), and Art. 3 complement each other, whereas others such as Art. 8 (Right to privacy), and Art. 10 (Freedom of expression), can in certain circumstances compete.

In R (Wright) v Home Office an asthmatic prisoner was locked in a cell and denied access to suitable medical treatment. The absence of treatment resulted in him dying as a result of an asthma attack. It was held that there had not only been a breach of Art. 2, but also that the pain and suffering endured at the time of the attack in combination with lack of medical treatment, constituted a violation of Art. 3.

Similarly in Keenan v UK a prisoner with established mental health issues and a known suicide risk, was placed in solitary confinement. He subsequently committed suicide. The ECtHR held that in violation of Art. 2, the prison authorities had failed to protect his life. In addition, the inadequate monitoring of his mental condition resulted in inhuman and degrading treatment.

Where people are in the custody of the state or are being arrested and are under the control of the police, they are unable to protect their own interests. Their treatment in such situation is liable to particular scrutiny. In Tomasi v France it was held that if a person enters police custody in a sound physical condition, but on release is found to have sustained injury, then the state must provide a plausible explanation.

However, in Caloc v France it was held that where a detainee resists arrest, seeks to escape or attacks others, then the use of force to restrain him will not violate Art. 3, even if an injury arises in the use of such treatment.

The UK's current legal regime for the treatment of prisoners is governed by statute, the Prison Act 1952, and subordinate legislation, the Prison Rules 1999. These must now be interpreted in accordance with the Convention. In Napier v The Scottish Ministers a prisoner was detained in grossly insanitary conditions, which exacerbated his eczema. The Scottish Court held that the applicant's treatment was in violation of Art. 3.

A review of the effect of the Napier decision is useful. It is noted that the passing of the HRA has provided prisoners with a mechanism to challenge prison rules and practices on the basis that they subject prisoners to inhuman or degrading treatment. Nevertheless, despite the absolute nature of Art. 3, the wide variety of differing practices across Europe in respect of sentencing, security and prison resources, may result in the ECtHR giving a wide margin of appreciation on the application of Art. 3 in this area.

It is felt that the specific circumstances relevant to Napier was a significant factor in the Court arriving at its decision, such as the applicant's skin condition and the fact that he was being held on remand. Nevertheless, in Wainwright v UK the ECtHR appeared to retreat from giving a wide interpretation to Art. 3 as suggested by Napier. Here, the applicant was strip searched in humiliating circumstances whilst visiting a relative on remand. It was agreed that the search had not been carried out in accordance with the Prison Rules 1999. The ECtHR held that the manner of the search violated the applicant's right to respect for private and family life under Art. 8. Even so, the ECtHR held that the treatment was not inhuman or degrading, as it did not reach the minimum level of severity prohibited by Art. 3.

A major criticism of the HRA was its failure to incorporate Art. 13. This imposes a duty on a member State to provide a remedy for violation of a convention right. The UK's argument against incorporation of this Article, is that the HRA itself gives effect to Art. 13 by establishing a scheme under s2(1) HRA under which convention rights can be raised and remedied before UK courts.

However, a violation of Art. 3 by a UK public authority may in several situations present no effective remedy for the victim. In Osman v UK , the police's blanket immunity against liability for negligence constituted a breach of Art. 6 and Art. 13.

The matter was further considered in Z v UK where four children suffered abuse at the hands of their parents for several years, of which the local authority were aware. The ECtHR held that the local authority was in breach of Art. 3 as it had failed in its positive obligation to protect the children from inhuman and degrading treatment. There was also held to be a breach of Art. 13, because the applicants did not have available to them a mechanism for establishing a breach of their Art. 3 rights. As a consequence, they had been denied an effective remedy in respect of their complaints.

The incorporation of Art. 3 has achieved significant effect. Whereas before the HRA, Art. 3 merely had persuasive influence, incorporation has resulted in the Article being directly applicable within the UK. As an absolute right incapable of derogation, the meaning and application of Art. 3 has been adapted to cover new and enhanced ideals of human rights protection.

The Case of Ireland afforded a comprehensive definition of what constituted ill-treatment for the purposes of Art. 3, and provided early clarification of the thresholds for inhuman and degrading treatment. Before the HRA, UK Courts were not obliged to follow ECtHR case law, and this stymied the domestic effect of the same. Under s2 HRA, UK courts now have a duty to take into account case law of the ECtHR and the ECmHR.

However, s2 HRA does not impose a duty of binding precedent of ECtHR decisions upon UK courts, and it is submitted that had s2 imposed such a duty, then this would have enhanced the domestic protection of human rights. The argument against this, is that as a "living instrument", ECtHR case law may require to be reconsidered in light of changing circumstances.

With regard to deportation, the Cases of Chahal and Soering have shown that the UK is under a positive duty to prevent a breach of Art. 3, even where the threat of violation emanates from a foreign country. The Napier Case has shown the potential effect that Art. 3 has on UK prison conditions, and the Cases of Tyrer and Campbell & Cosans have led to a ban on corporal punishment in UK schools..

Art. 3 continues to be interpreted widely as to the forms of treatment it covers. It has been used to bring human rights within its scope, which were not originally envisaged. The possibility of sexual discrimination falling within its ambit, was considered in Smith & Grady v UK. Similarly, in East Africa Asians v UK the ECtHR was invited to consider whether racially discriminatory treatment on the part of the UK Immigration Authority, was sufficiently degrading so as to constitute an Art 3 violation.

It is therefore submitted that notwithstanding its absolute nature, Art. 3 is a highly flexible Convention right, and in several areas has highlighted a deficiency in domestic UK law. The HRA's incorporation of the Article, together with the large body of ECtHR case law which UK courts must now take into account, has resulted in a significant protection of human rights in this area. The Article's boundaries continue to be extended, and the development of its interpretation will ensure continuity of its impact.

A frequent Article alleged to have been breached is Article 8 of the Act. Article 8 confers on all individuals the right to respect for his private and family life and his correspondence. The article also states that there shall be no interference by a public authority with the exercise of this right except such as is in accordance with the law and is necessary in a democratic society in the interests of national security, public safety or the economic wellbeing of the country, for the prevention of disorder or crime, for the protection of health and morals, or for the protection of the rights and freedoms of others.

The rights to a private and family life have in recent times been expanded to provide protection for the rights of transsexuals. Since the inception of the Human Rights Act there has been a greater acceptance of same sex couples and also recognition of the rights of the individual to undergo gender reassignment treatment so that they can become the person they feel they truly are on the inside. In the past anyone undergoing gender reassignment operations where frowned upon and could not acquire any legal recognition of their new gender. A man could in all sense and purposes have undergone all the necessary treatment so that in physical appearance he had been transformed into a female, but in law would still not be recognised as a female.

Transgender males or females were not entitled to have their birth certificate amended or altered in any way to reflect the change they had undergone. On the face of it, it could be argued that as the transsexuals can chose to be called by whatever name they so desire, that there is no need for the formality in having the birth certificate amended to reflect these changes. This argument is fine until such a time as the transsexual needs to produce of identity for such things as passports, driving licences, medical treatment and marriages or when applying for new employment.

It could also be extremely difficult if the transsexual gets arrested for a crime and sentenced to prison. If the male has had a gender reassignment so that he has now become a she if the transsexual were to be sentenced to a period of time in prison should he be sent to a male or a female prison. The problem also arises when prisoners need to be searched.

On the face of it the obvious solution would be to send the transsexual to a female prison, however in reality this may not be the decision of the judge in these cases. When the accused person is brought before the judge all forms of identity that would be presented to the judge would record the accused's sex as male. This could mean effectively that the court would disregard the outward appearance of the defendant and look to the gender recorded at birth in deciding which establishment the defendant should be sent to if their guilt is proven in court.

Since the establishment of the Act movement has headed towards a greater acceptance of the fact that those who have committed themselves to having gender reassignment treatment are so determined and set on fully becoming the sex they truly feel they were meant to be at birth that if allowed they would change totally to the opposite gender. For this to be complete, they would argue, that legislation should evolve to the extent that there is a wider acceptance of gender change couples and that they should be allowed to re-register their own birth. Recent changes in the law now allow transsexuals to re-register their births under their new identity so that they are then recognised in law as the sex they have chosen to be recognised as. Under the Gender Recognition Act 2004 those who have undergone gender reassignment will now have the right to re-register so that they can have a birth certificate the fully represents the gender they now are. There are certain criteria they have to meet to be allowed to do this but so long as they meet the specifications re-registration will be allowed.

Prior to the above mentioned Act several cases were brought before both the English courts and the European Court for Human Rights were those who had undergone reassignment were seeking the right to re-register. Those taken to the ECHR brought their claims on the grounds that refusing them the right to have a birth certificate that reflected their new gender was a breach of Article 8. In Sheffield and Horsham v. The United Kingdom, Ms Sheffield claimed that her right to privacy was breached because she had to disclose her original sex when she attended court to stand surety for a friend and when applying for car insurance. She was also ordered to divorce her wife before she was entitled to have surgery to change her sex. After the operation she was denied access to her daughter as the court decided it was not in the best interests of the child for her to have contact with a transsexual. At the time this case was brought before the ECHR the UK were still refusing to allow transsexuals to re-register and unfortunately for the plaintiff the ECHR refused to find that a breach of Article 8 had been proven thereby denying her the right to insist on re-registration. In the light of the new legislation Ms Sheffield would now be entitled to re-register.

A case decided in 1997 has extended the rights under Article 8 to cover protection of the countryside. In Britton v Secretary of State the court held that "private and family life" therefore encompasses not only the home but also the surroundings. This could effectively mean that Article 8 (2) would also apply where a listed building or a conservation area is affected, enabling people to demand respect for the special interest of the conservation area in which they live or nearby listed buildings as a human right.

A further area in which Article 8 has been invoked concerns the rights of people brought up in care to have access to the records held about them. In Gaskin v. UK the plaintiff claimed to have been abused whilst in care and was requesting access to the records held about him by Liverpool Social Services. Garvin was granted partial access with Liverpool social services claiming that confidentiality owed to third party contributors prohibited full disclosure. After exhausting all avenues in the English courts Gaskin took his case to the ECHR. The court there held that Article 8 had been breached in this case as there had been no independent appeal body to which Gaskin could have taken his case. They also held that it was a breach of Gaskin's right to a family life not to allow him access to his case records as Gaskin would have been provided with full details of his family background had he been brought up by his birth parents. Gaskin's case caused further impact on UK legislation with the Data Protection Act now containing special provisions whereby social services records are accessible by people formerly in public care irrespective of whether the records are kept electronically or within a paper-based filing system.

Following from the above decision it would seem fair to suggest that the withholding of information about medical treatment and denial of patients' rights to see their medical records could also be seen as a breach of Article 8. There could also be further claims for breach of Article 8 on the grounds of informed consent not being properly obtained. This might arise where a piece of information about the particular treatment is withheld thereby denying the patient to make a fully informed choice as to whether they wanted the treatment or not. It is not suggested that every patient should be given every single detail of their treatment or told of every possible complication that might occur, but doctors should ensure that sufficient information is supplied so that the patient can make a properly informed choice.

Article 8 has been further extended in respect of medical treatment to cover the rights of parents under Article 8 to be involved in important decisions concerning the treatment of their children.

When the Human Rights Act first came into inception psychiatrists were concerned about the impact the Act might have on their ability to treat the patients. Since its introduction into the legal system several psychiatric patients have challenged their treatment under Article 8. In the case of J.T. v. United Kingdom the claimant appealed against her inability to change her designated nearest relative. She alleged that preventing her from doing this violated her right to a private life which was upheld by the ECHR, thereby allowing her to nominate a new nearest relative.

Another case involving a mental health patient claiming a breach of Article 8 was Herczegfalvy v Austria. In this particular case the plaintiff challenged the opening of his correspondence by the curator of the institution as being a breach of Article 8. The ECHR held that this was indeed a breach and that the only way that a breach could be avoided would be for all correspondence in future to be opened in the presence of the plaintiff.

Case law has also extended the right to privacy to cover that right within the workplace too. In Halford v UK the ECHR held that the tapping of a telephone in the workplace was a breach of Article 8 unless the employer warned the employee that they intended to do so. The ECHR accepted that there are times when a breach of Article 8 is necessary to protect the rights and freedom of others. They also accepted that the monitoring of emails may be justified if the purpose is to ensure that offensive emails are not being sent to other employees. The Interception of Communications Regulations 2000 authorise employers to monitor staff e-mails, internet use and even phone calls at work, provided employers have a 'lawful' business purpose and that they make 'all reasonable efforts' to inform users of the monitoring.

In 1997 the Dixons Group brought an action against the BBC alleging a breach of their right to privacy when they secretly filmed sales transactions at their stores for a watchdog program. Whilst the judges were quick to point out that Article 8 does not extend to companies they did agree that there had been an infringement of the companies' privacy and that the infringement had been unwarranted. A later judicial review of the decision applied for by the BSC again stated that Article 8 did not apply to companies, but still held that there had been an unwarranted infringement of Dixon's privacy and the BSC had the power to deal with the complaint lodged by Dixon's and should have done so. The reasoning behind the ECHR decision that the infringement was unwarranted was that those doing the filming had not properly researched Dixon's before filming. This was evident by the fact that the filming failed to reveal any mis-selling which was the aim of the crew doing the filming.

The use of CCTV was raised in the case of Peck v. The United Kingdom. In this particular case the claimant was caught on CCTV in his local area attempting to commit suicide. Whilst the Commission accepted that the use of CCTV should not be challenged as a breach of Article 8 as a right in this particular instance the releasing of the footage to the BBC for use in a documentary showing how CCTV can help prevent and detect crime did amount to a breach of Article 8 as it specifically identified the claimant. The claimant was clearly seen on the footage cutting himself with a knife. The Commission held breached his right to privacy. The Commission did point out that if the claimant's image had been obscured so that his identity could not be revealed then there would have been no such breach. The Commission also stated that where the images of offenders were not obscured out but the intention of showing the footage was an appeal to the general public to help identify perpetrators of crimes there would be no breach of the right to privacy as the filming was in the public interest.

In 2000 Sultan Kahn brought an action against the United Kingdom claiming that the use of covert surveillance equipment by the police was an infringement of Article 8. In this instance the ECHR held that there had been a violation of Article 8 as at the time that the action was brought there was no statutory system to regulate the use of covert listening devices. The Home Office guidelines at that time were not legally binding nor directly accessible by the public. The Court therefore found that there was no basis in law for the interference in the claimant's private life and correspondence and a breach of Article 8 was substantiated.

There have been a number of cases in the United Kingdom brought by people who are incarcerated in prison claiming that the denial of conjugal rights whilst they are incarcerated is a breach of

Article 8, their right to a family life. The leading case of Mellor, R (on the application of) v Secretary Of State for Home Department held that there had been no infringement of Article 8 by the denying of conjugal rights to the plaintiff. They held that his demise was of his own making and that it was his unlawful actions that had led to his incarceration and ultimately his right to a family life. They held that the refusal of the prison service to allow conjugal rights in this case could be justified for the prevention of disorder or crime. Miss Rose in this case also highlighted that whereas she accepted that Article 8 guaranteed the tight to a private and family life and the right to marry and found a family it did not give any right to create a family by the conception of a child.

It is obvious from all of the above that since the introduction of the Human Rights Act into UK legislation there have been many times in which the rights provided by Article 8 have been challenged. Some of the cases illustrated above show that there has been a change in attitude towards acceptance of the rights of individuals. As highlighted above one of the most significant areas of change has evolved around transsexuals, although in roads are now being made into allowing same sex couples to marry.

The Civil Partnership Act 2004 which came into force on 5 December 2005 was an attempt by the UK government to allow same sex couples to undergo civil ceremonies similar to marriage ceremonies, thereby recognising them in law as a couple. This status is now protected against discrimination by virtue of the Equality Act 2010. The case of Wilkinson v Kitzinger & Ors was an attempt by a same sex couple to have their marriage in Vancouver recognised fully in the United Kingdom. The UK courts found that there right to a private life did not require the state to recognise their marriage. The UK courts held that for a foreign marriage to be recognised in the UK it had to be legal, recognised in the country in which it was executed, and that nothing in the country's law restricted their freedom to marry. The couple argued that their marriage did fill this criterion but the UK courts held that in the UK same sex marriages cannot be legally entered into. The UK was prepared to accept that under the Civil Partnership Act 2004 the couple could rightly be classified as civil partners. The couple rejected this and asked the courts to recognise their marriage in the same way it would recognise a heterosexual marriage. The courts rejected their assertion that not recognising their marriage in the same way as for a heterosexual couple was a breach of Article 8. They upheld the decision of the United Kingdom courts that as same sex marriages in the UK were not legally allowed and that the couple had the option to be deemed as civil partners there was no infringement of their rights to a family life.

The law on same sex marriages has since evolved to provide full recognition of the same. Consequently the Marriage (Same Sex Couples) Act 2013, provides full status to same sex marriages in the same manner as conventional marriages.

Since the Human Rights Act has been in operation there have been many changes brought about in the realms of the laws of privacy and the rights to a family life. The traditional family is now extending to cover same sex couples and transsexuals. Privacy has been extended beyond the boundaries of the family home and been taken into the area surrounding the family home as well as in the workplace. Most of these changes have been brought about by actions of claimants who feel that their right to privacy and a family life has been breached.

Chapter 5 – Collective agreements

The right to organise industrial action, is an important component of a free society. It is arguable that the past thirty years has witnessed an assault on UK trade union rights to the extent that our employment laws, remain woefully short of accepted UN and even EU norms.

Prior to 1979 there had been a substantial period of collective laissez-faire in relation to industrial relations. This meant that so long as the parties to a dispute were acting peacefully and in furtherance of a legitimate trade dispute, the law would not interfere in such dispute.

Unlike many other jurisdictions, UK law does not provide workers with a positive right to organise or engage in industrial action. Indeed, at common law, strike action constitutes a repudiatory breach of contract. In Taff Vale Railway Co v ASRS the HL held that the trade union could be sued in tort and that its assets could be taken in satisfaction of the judgment.

Taff Vale resulted in significant agitation leading to the enactment of the Trade Disputes Act 1906 ("the TDA"). This Act is considered to be a landmark in trade union legislation as it is effectively a precursor to the modern era.

The TDA provided a trade union with blanket immunity against an action in tort. It also gave immunity from liability for conspiracy and inducement of breach of contract to union officials, provided their actions were "acts done in contemplation or furtherance of a trade dispute".

The TDA remained in force until repealed by the Industrial Relations Act 1971 ("the IRA") which was passed by the short lived Heath government. The subsequent Wilson government repealed the IRA 1971, and restored the structure established by the 1906 Act.

In 1979, the Thatcher government placed reform of industrial relations as a centrepiece of its agenda. It rejected previous consensus about the management of industrial relations, and during the period 1979-97, initiated a process of regulation of industrial action by reference to its protected purposes and scope of procedure.

The Thatcher government's legislative programme has attracted significant criticism. The taking of industrial action will invariably result in the commission of at least one common law tort. These torts are often referred to as "economic torts", and have been developed by the courts in a piecemeal fashion, often in the context of liability for industrial action.

A term can be incorporated into a contract of employment from a collective agreement either expressly or impliedly. Express implication can come from the parties agreeing in writing that all or part of a collective agreement is binding upon them. In relation to implied incorporation each case will be decided on its particular facts. One of the factors which the court may consider is the degree of relevance of the provision in the collective agreement to the particular employee, previous custom and practice will also be relevant.

Consequently, it is important to analyse against what the law is protecting, and discuss the sources of potential liability.

An inducement to breach a contact occurs in circumstances where a trade union has induced its members into breaching their individual contracts, thereby resulting in damage to their employer. The tort was initially recognised in Lumley v Gye. It has subsequently been divided into direct and indirect inducement.

In the context of industrial action, the Lumley Case was affirmed by the HL in South Wales Miners' Federation v Glamorgan Coal Co Ltd , which confirmed that the inducing party must be aware of the existence of the affected contract.

Indirect inducement occurs in circumstances where the inducing party effects an unlawful act which results in a breach of a third party contract. This can occur in circumstances where industrial action results in an employer being unable to fulfil a supply contract with a third party. Indirect manifestation was first recognised in DC Thompson & Co v Deakin. The CA stated that for the tort to be established it was necessary to show that the inducing party knew of the existence of the contract, persuaded employees to procure a breach of their employment contracts and that a breach occurred.

The tort of interference with a contract or with a business occurs in circumstances where there has been interference with trade or business by virtue of an unlawful act, culminating in damage to the employer's trade or business, although the interference with the contract falls short of actual breach. Such interference must be deliberate, direct and effected with knowledge of the contract.

In Torquay Hotel Co Ltd v Cousins an oil supply contract failed as a result of industrial action. Although due to the presence of a force majeure clause in the supply contract there was no breach, Denning LJ suggested that there could still be liability on the part of the trade union for preventing or hindering performance of the original contract.

The tort of intimidation consists of coercion or threats by unlawful means. The tortfeasor must intend to cause harm to the claimant and the act must have that effect. A direct threat to the employer causing damage is known as two-party intimidation. A direct threat to another resulting in damage to the employer is known as three-party intimidation.

In Rookes v Barnard a non-union employee was dismissed as a result of a trade union threatening strike action against his employer. The HL accepted that the tort could embrace threats to breach employment contracts on the taking of industrial action. It was noted that existing immunities under the TDA were not applicable.

The tort of economic duress is an extension of intimidation. It occurs when one party is in such a dominant position that the other party has no alternative but to accede to an unlawful demand.

In Universe Tankships Inc of Monrovia v ITWF the HL was prepared to accept the Claimant's argument that due to economic duress on the part of the union, they had been placed in a situation in which they had no practical alternative but to agree to the union's demands.

The tort of conspiracy may take either of two forms and must involve a combination of two or more persons. Conspiracy by lawful means to injure, occurs where the infliction of harm on a third party is the predominant purpose.

Conspiracy to commit an unlawful act or use unlawful means is committed where there is an intention to injure the third party by the employment of means which are unlawful in themselves. Consequently, in Rookes v Barnard the three union officials were held to have committed two torts, namely intimidation and conspiracy to use unlawful means.

In Crofter Hand Woven Harris Tweed Co v Veitch the HL held that there was an appropriate defence if the union officials were acting to protect their own legitimate interests. Therefore a genuine reason for industrial action, in accordance with the union's objects would not constitute the tort in these circumstances.

The tort of inducing a breach of Statutory duty is of particular concern to employees of public services, where industrial action may result in their employer being in breach of a Statutory obligation.

In Meade v L.B. Haringey the CA suggested, obiter, that school closures as a result of industrial action, could result in liability on the part of the union by virtue of inducing the local authority to breach its Statutory obligation to provide educational facilities.

The scope of statutory immunity protection for union officials is provided by s219(1) Trade Union and Labour Relations (Consolidation) Act 1992 ("TULRCA"), which provides that an act done in contemplation or furtherance of a trade dispute is not actionable in tort on the ground only that it induces another person to break and/or threaten to break, interfere or induce another to either break a contract or interfere with its performance.

Section 219(1) provides immunity against the torts of interference with the contract, inducement and intimidation. Similar immunity against the tort of conspiracy by lawful means is provided by s219(2) TULRCA.

It should be noted that TULRCA is effectively a consolidating statute. Hence s219 TULRCA consolidated the corresponding provisions of the Employment Act 1982. Section 219 defines those torts which form the subject matter of protection, rather than provide comprehensive immunity. It is arguable that this method of listing torts means that those organising industrial action will be vulnerable to new torts being created.

It has already been seen how in Rookes v Barnard the HL outflanked the Statutory immunities by applying the tort of intimidation to an industrial dispute. Therefore s219 remains vulnerable to the common law creating new economic torts which do not enjoy existing Statutory immunity.

In order to ensure engagement of the Statutory immunities, the proposed industrial action must fall within the "golden formula" - It must be "in contemplation or furtherance of a trade dispute". Section 244(1) TULRCA defines a "trade dispute" as a "dispute between workers and their employer" which relates "wholly or mainly" to a number of specifically defined matters.

There are seven listed matters defined in s244(1)(a) to s244(1)(g) which cover the definition of what constitutes a "trade dispute". These cover most workplace disputes including terms and conditions of employment, engagement or termination, discipline and trade union activities.

Therefore, if the subject matter of the industrial action does not fall within the s244(1) definition of a "trade dispute", it will fall outside the ambit of the golden formula. The action will become unlawful and the Statutory immunities will not apply.

Until the Employment Act 1982, the definition of a trade dispute was much wider. Prior to this Act, a lawful trade dispute need only be "connected with" one of the listed matters, and would only be unlawful if wholly unconnected.

In BBC v Hearn an injunction was granted against the union which had threatened industrial action in protest against apartheid. It was held that the proposed industrial action had nothing to do with the terms and conditions of the workers involved.

Since 1982, the dispute must relate "wholly or mainly" to one of the s244(1) TULRCA listed matters. In most disputes, this is fairly obvious. However, where the dispute has a quasi-political or other non-industrial purpose, then the common law will apply a "predominant purpose" test in order to determine whether s244(1) applies.

In Mercury Communications Ltd v Scott-Garner an industrial dispute over the privatisation of telecommunications, was held by the CA to fall outside the Statutory definition of a trade dispute. The CA decided that the predominant purpose of the dispute related to the union's opposition to privatisation of the telecommunications industry.

Conversely in L.B. Wandsworth v NASUWT a teachers' dispute over incorporation of the national curriculum, was held to be wholly or mainly connected to the Statutory definition, on the basis that it mainly related to terms and conditions of employment.

The Employment Act 1982 further narrowed a trade dispute definition to the extent that it must constitute "a dispute between workers and their employer". At the time this was an important limitation, because it excluded from the Statutory definition, disputes between workers including demarcation and inter-union disputes.

In UC London Hospitals NHS Trust v UNISON a dispute over the transfer of terms and conditions on a potential business transfer, was held not to constitute a valid trade dispute, on the basis that the dispute related to employees of an unidentified employer.

Central to the operation of the golden formula is the fact that the industrial action must be "in contemplation or furtherance" of the dispute. This involves consideration of the purpose of the dispute and its timing.

The issue of purpose was considered in Express Newspapers v McShane. The HL held that with regard to the dispute's purpose, a subjective test would be applicable. Hence there would be immunity if the union official honestly believed that the action might further the cause of those taking part.

Timing was considered in Bent's Brewery Co Ltd v Hogan . Here, a potential industrial dispute was held to fall outside the definition on the basis that it was not in existence or sufficiently imminent. However in Health Computing Ltd v Meek the submission of circulars by a union to its membership was held to be sufficiently proximate to a contemplated dispute.

Trade Union Liability is covered under s4 TDA. This provides a trade union with blanket immunity against an action in tort. Fundamental change was enacted by the Thatcher government by virtue of the Employment Act 1982.

In order to enjoy immunity both the union and its officials must now fall within the ambit of the golden formula. A union's blanket immunity has been lost. The union is still capable of enjoying immunity under the golden formula, but on the same terms as afforded to its officials under s219 TULRCA.

It is arguable that we are almost back to the Taff Vale position, where in the event of an immunity failing to apply, the union itself can be held liable. Nevertheless, partial protection against potential union insolvency is afforded by s22 TULRCA, which specifies a maximum limit of damages depending upon the size of the union membership.

A trade union will now incur statutory vicarious responsibility for the actions of its members, where such act was authorised or endorsed by one of three classes of persons. These are defined in s20(2), and include the union president, general secretary, any union committee, any other official of the union, and, any person empowered by the union rules to do so, whether or not such person is employed by the union.

The case of Heatons Transport Ltd V TGWU involved the concept of implied authorisation under the short lived IRA 1971. Here, the HL held that a shop steward had general implied authority and discretion to act on the union's behalf.

It is possible for the union to "repudiate" unauthorised industrial action, and thereby escape vicarious liability. Section 21 TULRCA provides detailed guidelines as to an effective repudiation which must be effected promptly and in writing to every member of the union taking part in the proposed action.

In Express & Star v NGA the union was held liable for unofficial industrial action, despite instructing members not to participate, on the basis that regional union officials were still participating in the dispute.

The primary means by which an employer seeks to challenge industrial action is by way of application for an interim injunction. This is a discretionary equitable remedy, and as a result of American Cyanamid v Ethicon Ltd a court must be satisfied that there is a "serious question to be tried". An interim injunction will be directed at the tortfeasor, and lasts up to the full trial.

Section 221(2) TULRCA provides that in the determination of whether to grant an interim injunction, the court shall have regard to whether the matter in question constitutes an act taken in contemplation or furtherance of a trade dispute, and, whether in the event of the matter proceeding to a full trial, the tortfeasor is likely to succeed in establishing a s219 statutory immunity.

An injunction can be coupled with an award for damages. Breach of an injunction constitutes contempt of court. Prior to the Employment Act 1982, industrial dispute injunctions were usually directed at union officials. However, the removal of a union's blanket immunity, effectively means that injunctions are now capable of being addressed to both a union and its officials.

In Mercury Communications Ltd v Scott-Gardner and the POEU one of the reasons why the court was prepared to grant an injunction, was due to the fact that the available statutory financial remedy under s22 TULRCA would have been insufficient. Had the strike gone ahead, then the losses incurred by the employer would have exceeded the statutory remedy.

The Thatcher government also expanded the category of potential claimants entitled to seek an injunction against the taking of unlawful industrial action. Section 62 TULRCA enables an individual union member to seek an injunction, if he is required to take part in an unballoted dispute.

Section 235A enables an individual to bring a claim where the effect of an unlawful action prevents or delays the supply of goods or services to him. In P v NAS/UWT the HL rejected an excluded pupil's claim against his school's teaching union, on the basis that the dispute was lawfully balloted and related to terms and conditions of employment.

It is important to note that protection afforded by the statutory immunities only applies to a "lawful" trade dispute. The Thatcher government proceeded on a legislative programme which effectively confined the scope of industrial action by reference to its protected purposes and initiating procedure.

These are known as the "claw-back" provisions of ss222 to 234A TULRCA, which enable removal of the statutory immunities and restoration of common law liability. They include, inter alia, the requirement for balloting, regulation of picketing and a restriction on secondary action.

Ballots and notices of industrial action are covered under the Trade Union Act 1984. Industrial action is only lawful in the event of a secret ballot being held to demonstrate general support. Consequently, s226 TULRCA provides that a union should not call for industrial action unless such action has the support of a ballot within the meaning of TULRCA, and, that the relevant employer has been given proper notice of such ballot.

Compliance with s226 TULRCA is a condition precedent for the dispute to constitute protected industrial action. In the event of there either being no ballot, or a procedurally defective ballot, then the dispute will become unlawful and statutory immunities lost.

The union needs to initially identify which members are to be balloted. Section 227(1) provides that when it holds its ballot, the union must allow a vote to all those members which it is reasonable for the union at the time of the ballot, for it to believe will be induced to take part.

The ballot constituency is "the workplace", and under s228 if the voters have different workplaces, then there should be a separate ballot for each workplace. In certain circumstances, s228A allows for an aggregated ballot across more than one workplace. In University of Central England vg NALGO it was held that an aggregate ballot could be held across different workplaces even where there was a different employer at the other workplace.

Section 229 TULCRA specifies the minimum requirements of the contents of the ballot paper. In particular, 229(2) provides that the ballot paper must include at least one of two questions, requiring a "yes" or "no" answer, as to whether the voter is prepared to take part in a strike, or whether he wishes to take part in industrial action short of a strike.

In London Underground Ltd v NUR the ballot paper was held to be defective in that union members were asked to vote by reference to matters which were not existing at the time of the dispute. However, L.B. Wandsworth v NAS is authority that a union is entitled to substantiate its case for the proposed industrial action in the drafting of the question.

Section 230(2) provides that the ballot must be conducted by post submitted to the voter's home address. Section 230(1)(a) states that each voter is entitled to conduct his vote without interference or constraint imposed by his union. In RJB Mining Ltd v NUM it was held that "interference or constraint" implies improper interference or constraint. However, in L.B. Newham v NALGO the CA held that the union was entitled to be partisan.

Pursuant to s226(2) a simple majority of the voters is sufficient to validate industrial action. Under s234(1), the industrial action must commence within four weeks of the ballot, or where the parties agree, a period not exceeding eight weeks.

It is arguable that the balloting provisions are unfair and costly to trade unions. Significant amounts of union resources are being expended on conducting ballots, and in defending technical arguments on the result.

A Code of Practice provides additional guidance on the conduct of the ballot. Failure to comply with its provisions can be used as evidence of the unlawfulness of the ballot. One of the more controversial aspects of the ballot and notice provisions, was the introduction of a requirement on the part of a union to give notice and information about not only the ballot, but also the proposed industrial action, to the affected employer.

Section 234A(1) provides that the union must give at least seven days notice to the employer prior to the commencement of industrial action. If not, then such action is unprotected.

Although the rational behind the introduction of the above provisions was to avoid random strike action, it is submitted that this is effectively a constraint on union activity, as an employer is now provided with a mechanism to make arrangements in preparation for forthcoming industrial action.

The Thatcher and subsequent Major governments introduced the balloting and notice provisions in order to prevent industrial action being called by a few union officials who did not enjoy majority support. This has become a "two-edged" sword. A tactical advantage in favour of the union is created, where a ballot enjoys the overwhelming support of the membership, by increasing pressure on the employer to settle.

Picketing per se can constitute a breach of several of the above economic torts. It is also capable of giving rise to the additional torts of trespass, nuisance and harassment. Further, there is the potential of criminal liability for obstruction and breach of the peace.

Section 2 TDA initially established a Statutory immunity. The scope of immunity for picketing is now governed by s220 TULRCA. The Thatcher government sought to further regulate the conduct of picketing by introducing a Code of Practice, which inter alia attempted to limit the number of pickets at an entrance or exit from a workplace.

Although the Code is not in itself legally binding, it is admissible in evidence. As with the Code on balloting, the Code of Practice can be taken into account when considering the legality of the picket.

Section 220 provides that it is lawful for a person in contemplation or furtherance of a trade dispute to attend at or near his own place of work for the purpose of peacefully obtaining or communicating information, or peacefully persuading a person to work or abstain from working.

It should be noted that s220 does not confer a right to picket, but merely protects attendance at a workplace for the purposes of peaceful picketing. In Broome v DPP the HL held that the purpose of an individual picket blocking the passage of a lorry, was to obstruct rather than peacefully persuade.

A picket which takes place in breach of s220, will result in the loss of immunity from the economic torts, as well any additional torts specific to the picket. The usual remedy of an injunction and damages, is available.

Nevertheless, it is submitted that peaceful picketing constitutes an exercise of the rights of freedom of expression and freedom of assembly . In Gate Gourmet v TGWU it was recognised that Art. 11 of the Convention may have established a "right to picket" insofar as peaceful assembly is concerned.

The Thatcher and Major governments additionally sought to tackle the issue of secondary picketing. This expression applied to striking workers picketing a connected workplace, and also, to non-workers who out of solidarity joined a picket line of workers. Unlike primary picketing, secondary picketing is not permitted under s220, and therefore the Statutory immunities will cease to apply.

The definition of secondary action is contained within s224(2) TULRCA. It occurs when a person either induces, interferes or threatens another person to breach an employment contract, and, the employer to such contract is not a party to the dispute.

The restriction on secondary action arose out of the Employment Act 1980. As a result of s224(1) TULRCA, if an industrial action falls within the definition of secondary action, it is unlawful and the Statutory immunities will be lost. The main exception is secondary action during the course of lawful picketing as defined by s220.

The prohibition on secondary action is a serious constraint on the organisation of industrial action, as in many cases the ambit of lawful industrial action will be determined by the corporate structure of the relevant employer.

During the Thatcher and Major administrations, several public utilities were either privatised or broken-up into smaller units, such as gas, railways, electricity and water. As a consequence, industrial action by workers of one privatised unit in favour of a dispute involving workers from another privatised unit, has been restricted.

The Thatcher government maintained that many of its reforms were introduced under the banner of "democratising" the workplace in favour of the individual worker. Hence it could be argued, that the incremental abolition of the closed shop commencing with the Employment Act 1980, was an attempt to protect an individual workers' right to decide whether to join a union in the first place.

It is also arguable that the balloting provisions encouraged "inclusivity" on the part of ordinary union members in the decision to commence industrial action. Nevertheless, it is submitted that once industrial action had been initiated, an individual worker has been placed in no better position than that of the union or its officials.

The position of an individual dismissed as a result of strike action, is dependent upon the status of the dispute. Where an employee participates in official industrial action which has been properly balloted and complies with requisite notice provisions, then such action becomes "protected".

In such situation the industrial action is both official and lawful. Consequently, s238A TULRCA provides that dismissal by the employer for taking part in the dispute during the first twelve weeks, will be automatically unfair.

In the event of official industrial action which is not protected, or, in the event of protected official action exceeding twelve weeks duration, then the situation is different. Here, s238 provides that an employee will have an ordinary unfair dismissal claim only if the employer has engaged in unfair "selectivity" on dismissal or re-engagement.

Where an employee is dismissed in connection with unofficial industrial action, he is deemed to have participated in an unlawful action. Pursuant to s237(1) he has no right to lodge a specific complaint for unfair dismissal by virtue of his participation. In addition, where a union undertakes official action to support a worker having been dismissed for taking unofficial action, such action is unlawful.

There is a perceived conception that the "Winter of Discontent", was the culmination of a period of economic disruption organised by workers and their unions, taking advantage of a collective laissez-faire approach to industrial relations.

The Thatcher administration set out to combat its perception of economic disruption by embarking on an incremental legislative programme designed to regulate what constituted lawful industrial action.

As a consequence, there is no doubt there that has been a decline in the number of industrial disputes since 1979. The decline in the number of disputes supports the contention that there is now a more balanced equilibrium between employer and worker. Even so, there are other factors which have contributed to this decline, such as the reduction in membership of the trade union movement, and the gradual change from a predominantly manufacturing to a service based economy.

In creating new causes of action by virtue of the "claw-back" provisions, it is submitted that the balance of power in an industrial dispute now appears to have been tilted in favour of the employer. There is now a much greater willingness on the part of employers to resort to legal sanctions when faced with disputes. In this respect, the Thatcher and Major legislative programmes failed to achieve an equitable equilibrium.

Chapter 6 – Discrimination

Domestic discrimination law has developed over more than 40 years since the first Race Relations Act in 1965. The domestic law was previously contained in the following legislation;
- Equal Pay Act 1970;
- Sex Discrimination Act 1975;
- Race Relations Act 1976;
- Disability Discrimination Act 1995;
- Employment Equality (Religion or Belief) Regulations 2003;
- Employment Equality (Sex Orientation) Regulations 2003;
- Employment Equality (Age) Regulations 2006;
- Equality Act 2006
- Equality Act (Sexual Orientation) Regulations 2007.

The Equality Act 2010 came into force during October 2010. The EA had two main purposes, namely, to harmonise discrimination law and to strengthen the law to support progress on equality. The EA 2010 brought together and restated most of the above enactments and a number of other related provisions. It harmonised all the former statutory provisions to give a single approach where appropriate. Virtually all of the former anti-discriminatory legislation has been repealed.

One of the principal aims of the EA was harmonisation of the existing strands of discrimination law. These were all brought together in s4 EA as protected characteristics: These are the grounds on which discrimination is deemed to be unlawful. The EA then goes onto define what is meant by each of these protected characteristics;
- Age (s5 EA) - This section establishes that where the EA refers to the protected characteristic of age, it means a person belonging to a particular age group. An age group includes people of the same age and people of a particular range of ages. Where people fall in the same age group they share the protected characteristic of age.

- Disability (s6 EA) - This section establishes who is to be considered as having the protected characteristic of disability and is a disabled person for the purposes of the Act. With Schedule 1 and regulations to be made under that Schedule, it will also establish what constitutes a disability. Where people have the same disability, they share the protected characteristic of disability.
- Gender reassignment (s7 EA) - This section defines the protected characteristic of gender reassignment for the purposes of the EA as where a person has proposed, started or completed a process to change his or her sex. A transsexual person has the protected characteristic of gender reassignment.
- Marriage and civil partnership (s8 EA) - This section defines the protected characteristic of marriage and civil partnership. People who are not married or civil partners do not have this characteristic. The section also explains that people who have or share the common characteristics of being married or of being a civil partner can be described as being in a marriage or civil partnership. A married man and a woman in a civil partnership both share the protected characteristic of marriage and civil partnership.
- Race (s9 EA) - This section defines the protected characteristic of race. For the purposes of the EA "race" includes colour, nationality and ethnic or national origins. The section explains that people who have or share characteristics of colour, nationality or ethnic or national origins can be described as belonging to a particular racial group. A racial group can be made up of two or more different racial groups.
- Religion or belief (s10 EA) - This section defines the protected characteristic of religion or religious or philosophical belief, which is stated to include for this purpose a lack of religion or belief. It is a broad definition in line with the freedom of thought, conscience and religion guaranteed by Article 9 of the ECHR.
- Sex (s11 EA) - This section is a new provision which explains that references in the Act to people having the protected characteristic of sex are to mean being a man or a woman, and that men share this characteristic with other men, and women with other women.

- Sexual orientation (s12 EA) - This section defines the protected characteristic of sexual orientation as being a person's sexual orientation towards: people of the same sex as him or her (in other words the person is a gay man or a lesbian); people of the opposite sex from him or her (the person is heterosexual); people of both sexes (the person is bisexual). It also explains that references to people sharing a sexual orientation mean that they are of the same sexual orientation.
- Pregnancy and Maternity (s18 EA) - This section defines the protected characteristic of pregnancy and maternity, and what it means to discriminate in the workplace because of a woman's pregnancy or pregnancy-related illness, or because she takes or tries to take maternity leave. The period during which protection from these types of discrimination is provided is the period of the pregnancy and any statutory maternity leave to which she is entitled.

A significant part of anti-discriminatory legislation in the UK has its origins from EU directives. An example is the Equal Treatment Directive. As a reminder, in certain circumstances, employees may rely directly on EU Directives, such as where these give better rights than domestic legislation. An employee may only rely on this "direct effect" principle however where their employer is a Member State. However the term "Member State" has been interpreted to include state employers such as local authorities. In addition, the Directive must be clear, precise, unconditional and unqualified for this provision to be relied on.

Whilst employees of private companies cannot rely on this provision, following the ECJ case of Francovich v Italian Republic 1992 IRLR 84, they may sue the state directly if it has failed to properly implement a directive and the individual has suffered damage.

In any event to date, where 'state' employees have successfully brought cases using the direct effect principle, consequent statutory changes apply to all employees both in the private and public sector. The Equal Treatment Directive only covers discrimination on the ground of sex. However, in some cases a decision based on the Directive's provisions will also affect the law relating to discrimination: An example of this approach can be seen in Marshall v Southampton & South-West Hampshire Area Health Authority (No. 2) 1993 IRLR 445.

Section 13 EA defines direct discrimination. This occurs where the reason for a person being treated less favourably than another is a protected characteristic listed in s4 EA. Section13(1) EA provides;

A person (A) discriminates against another person (B) if, because of a protected characteristic, A treats B less favourably than A treats or would treat others.

The section replaced the definitions of direct discrimination in previous legislation and is designed to provide a more uniform approach by removing the former specific requirement for the victim of the discrimination to have one of the protected characteristics of age, disability, gender reassignment and sex. Accordingly, it brings the position in relation to these protected characteristics into line with that for race, sexual orientation and religion or belief in the previous legislation.

However, a different approach applies where the reason for the treatment is marriage or civil partnership, in which case only less favourable treatment because of the victim's status amounts to discrimination. It must be the victim, rather than anybody else, who is married or a civil partner.

Section 14 EA provides for the discrimination prohibited by the Act to include direct discrimination because of a combination of two protected characteristics ("dual discrimination"). The protected characteristics which may be combined are age, disability, gender reassignment, race, religion or belief, sex and sexual orientation.

Section 14 EA provides that;

A person (A) discriminates against another (B) if, because of a combination of two relevant protected characteristics, A treats B less favourably than A treats or would treat a person who does not share either of those characteristics.

Previous legislation only allowed for claims alleging discrimination because of a single protected characteristic. This section allows those who have experienced less favourable treatment because of a combination of two relevant protected characteristics to bring a direct discrimination claim, such as where the single-strand approach may not succeed.

For a claim to be successful, the claimant must show that the less favourable treatment was because of the combination alleged, as compared with how a person who does not share either of the characteristics in the combination is or would be treated. A dual discrimination claim will not succeed where an exception or justification applies to the treatment in respect of either of the relevant protected characteristics.

The claimant does not have to show that a claim of direct discrimination in respect of each protected characteristic would have been successful if brought separately. A claimant is not prevented from bringing direct discrimination claims because of individual protected characteristics and a dual discrimination claim simultaneously (or more than one dual discrimination claim).

Section 19 EA defines indirect discrimination for the purposes of the Act. Sections 19(1) and 19(2) EA provide;

A person (A) discriminates against another (B) if A applies to B a provision, criterion or practice which is discriminatory in relation to a relevant protected characteristic of B's. (s19(1) EA).

For the purposes of subsection (1), a provision, criterion or practice is discriminatory in relation to a relevant protected characteristic of B's if-

• A applies, or would apply, it to persons with whom B does not share the characteristic,

• It puts, or would put, persons with whom B shares the characteristic at a particular disadvantage when compared with persons with whom B does not share it,

• It puts, or would put, B at that disadvantage, and

• A cannot show it to be a proportionate means of achieving a legitimate aim.

Consequently the EA uses the standard definition of indirect discrimination which occurs when a policy which applies in the same way for everybody has an effect which particularly disadvantages people with a protected characteristic. Where a particular group is disadvantaged in this way, a person in that group is indirectly discriminated against if he or she is put at that disadvantage, unless the person applying the policy can justify it.

Indirect discrimination can also occur when a policy would put a person at a disadvantage if it were applied. This means, for example, that where a person is deterred from doing something, such as applying for a job or taking up an offer of service, because a policy which would be applied would result in his or her disadvantage, this may also be indirect discrimination.

Indirect discrimination applies to all the protected characteristics, apart from pregnancy and maternity. A major departure from previous legislation is the extension of indirect discrimination to disability.

The wide approach taken with direct discrimination, has also been adopted with regard to harassment. As with direct discrimination, the victims of harassment do not have to possesss the protected characteristic themselves. Section 26 EA defines what is meant by harassment for the purposes of the Act and in essence there are three types of harassment.

- The first type, which applies to all the protected characteristics apart from pregnancy and maternity, and marriage and civil partnership, involves unwanted conduct which is related to a relevant characteristic and has the purpose or effect of creating an intimidating, hostile, degrading humiliating or offensive environment for the complainant or violating the complainant's dignity. (s26(1) EA).
- The second type is sexual harassment which is unwanted conduct of a sexual nature where this has the same purpose or effect as the first type of harassment. (s26(2) EA).
- The third type is treating someone less favourably because they have either submitted to or rejected sexual harassment, or harassment related to sex or gender reassignment. (s26(3) EA).

Previous legislation provided freestanding protection against harassment, but the first type of harassment described above was not defined in the same way for all the different protected characteristics to which it applied. In determining the effect of the unwanted conduct, courts and tribunals will continue to be required to balance competing rights on the facts of a particular case. For example this could include balancing the rights of freedom of expression (as set out in Article 10 of the European Convention on Human Rights) and of academic freedom against the right not to be offended in deciding whether a person has been harassed.

Section 27(1) EA defines what conduct amounts to victimization. It provides that;

A person (A) victimizes another person (B) if A subjects B to a detriment because A does a protected act, or, A belivies that B has done, or may do, a protected act.

Thus victimisation takes place where one person treats another badly because he or she in good faith done a "protected act". An example would be that of the victim taking or supported any action taken for the purpose of the EA. Section 27(1) also provides that victimisation takes place where one person treats another badly because he or she is suspected of having done this or of intending to do this. However it is significant, (and also a matter of "common sense"), that a person is not protected from victimisation under the EA, where that person maliciously makes or supports an untrue complaint.

This section replaces similar provisions in earlier legislation. Nevertheless, there is now a different approach in that it is no longer necessary to establish less favourable treatment. Hence it is no longer necessary to compare treatment of the victim with that of a person who has not made or supported a complaint under the Act.

Instructing and causing discrimination is now rendered unlawful by virtue of s111 EA. This section makes it unlawful for a person to instruct, cause or induce someone to discriminate against, harass or victimise another person, or to attempt to do so. Consequently, s111 provides a remedy not only for the recipient of the instruction, but also the intended victim. This applies whether or not the instruction is carried out, but only on the basis that the victim suffers a detriment as a result.

However, s111(7) EA provides that the prohibition only applies where the person giving the instruction is in a relationship with the recipient of the instruction in which discrimination, harassment or victimisation is prohibited. Section 111 EA replaces provisions in previous anti-discriminatory legislation. It extends protection to all protected characteristics in all areas covered by the Act and allows the Equality and Human Rights Commission to bring enforcement proceedings in relation to any action in breach of the section.

Positive action is not a new phenomenon. Previous legislation had addressed positive action. However, these applied to different protected characteristics in different ways. Furthermore, they were specific about the permitted types of positive action. Section 159 EA takes a different approach. In going further than previously permitted, the EA permits an employer to take a protected characteristic into consideration. This would apply when deciding who to recruit or promote, where people having the protected characteristic are at a disadvantage or are under-represented. Under the EA this can be done only where the candidates are as qualified as each other. This section is new. While previous legislation allowed employers to undertake a variety of positive action measures, for instance offering training and encouragement for certain forms of work, it did not allow employers to take any form of positive action at the actual point of recruitment or promotion.

Section 136 EA endeavours to harmonise the burden of proof provisions. Consequently, s136 provides that, in any claim where a person alleges discrimination, the burden of proving the case starts with the claimant. The Claimant initially needs to show facts, which in the absence of any other explanation, point to a breach having occurred. Once this has been established, then the burden shifts onto the respondent to show that the provisions of the EA were not breached.

The inescapable fact relating to pregnancy is that only women can become pregnant. Biology dictates that women only are physiologically able to carry an unborn child and then give birth. This for women and families alike is a potentially joyous occasion but one that also can cause real difficulty and stress.

In the twenty first century, women now form almost half of the labour market in the United Kingdom. Furthermore, the percentage of women, of working age, who are economically active, has substantially increased in the years since the early 1970s. On that basis, and bearing in mind the fact that pregnancy is one of the most natural events in any family's life, it would not, from a theoretical (and perhaps an ideological) perspective seem unrealistic (or unreasonable) for the law to provide comprehensive protection for pregnant women in the work place, both during and after pregnancy.

Employers, one would expect, often having families of their own, would be understanding and sympathetic to those needs of a pregnant woman. However, with pregnancy comes inevitable change and disruption. A woman may require time off work for antenatal appointments. She may suffer from illness during her pregnancy and inevitably, she will require time off for the birth of her child and then for a period of time thereafter.

For an employer who is simply concerned with his or her short-term business needs, this can be viewed as an inconvenient problem, which has to be addressed, and one, which requires time and resources to deal with; a distraction to the business ultimately leading to time being spent on non-profit making activities.

As such, a far too common experience for pregnant women is that of bullying, the loss of employment, loss of promotions and being faced with a negative and unsupportive attitude of an employer. One must accept also that a pregnant woman, in the work environment, is in a vulnerable, uncertain and anxious position. Significant time off will be required and with a child comes childcare responsibilities. Furthermore from a financial perspective, a child brings its own burden.

The employment relationship therefore, should be governed by a clear set of legal rules providing effective and accessible rights and remedies to pregnant women. Reality however paints an altogether different picture: This has been described as a complicated jigsaw of rights and responsibilities all operating at the same time in a legal vacuum.

The law in this area is unduly complex. It has evolved as part of equality legislation. The EA deals with the concepts of direct and indirect discrimination. Both involve comparisons between men and women. The concepts deal with both formal and substantive equality but in terms of pregnancy, has led to the vexing of lawyers and legal academics alike.

The very nature of equality deals with comparison. How then does the law, align pregnancy with equality given the fact that only women can fall pregnant? Against whom can the comparison apply?

Hence an evaluation should be undertaken on the evolution of the law relating to pregnancy and the influence of EU law in the form of the Equal Treatment Directive and the Pregnant Workers Directive.

In addition to the right of pregnant women not to be discriminated against on the ground of her sex, statute law has also developed to give specific rights to pregnant women. These are largely contained in the Employment Rights Act 1996 which, inter alia, provides that a woman (irrespective of the length of her continuous employment) who is dismissed for a reason relating to pregnancy shall be regarded as having been unfairly dismissed. Furthermore, Statutory Instruments, namely. Many women experience adverse treatment in the workplace both during and after pregnancy. This is indisputably unfair. Women experience treatment in the workplace that is unsafe and unlawful. However, despite the legal rules that are in place to counteract this, such treatment continues.

Pregnancy, (and the period after birth), brings of itself huge changes for women both physically and emotionally. At this time, a woman needs fair, safe and lawful treatment in the workplace and should this be lacking, an accessible and effective form of redress. This assignment will (drawing on research evidence) explore the possible reasons why the legal rules are inadequate in many respects leaving pregnant women vulnerable, stressed and exposed.

In order to appreciate the legal rules to counteract adverse treatment for pregnant women and complexities of the law in this area, it is essential to consider the how the law has developed and the way in which the courts have applied the law to situations involving the treatment of pregnant women. It is of critical importance to pregnant women to ensure their continuity of employment, both during and after pregnancy, should this be required.

The law on dismissal essentially has developed in two ways. First in treating dismissal on the grounds of pregnancy as sex discrimination and second in treating such dismissals as unfair.

Sex discrimination involves the comparison of the treatment of men and women in the workplace. Direct discrimination occurs where, on the grounds of her sex a woman is treated less favourably than he treats or would treat a man. Indirect discrimination occurs where, he applies to her a requirement or condition which he apples or would apply equally to a man but is such that the proportion of women who can comply is considerably smaller than the proportion of men who can comply with it. Furthermore, such indirect discrimination cannot be shown to be justified irrespective of sex and which is to her detriment because she cannot comply with it.

Applying the comparison on a literal basis however the courts in the case of Turley v Allders Department Stores Ltd held that dismissal due to pregnancy did not fall within the statutory definition of discrimination. This case was heard by the Employment Appeal Tribunal following appeal by Mrs Turley from the (then) Industrial Tribunal. The court considered the provisions of s1 of the SDA 1975 and made a distinction between a "woman" and a "pregnant woman". Bristow J stated that in applying the Act one must look at men and women and see that they are not treated unequally because they are men and women. "You have to compare like with like. So, in the case of the pregnant woman there is an added difficulty in the application of subsection (1). Suppose that to dismiss her for pregnancy is to dismiss her on the ground of her sex. In order to see if she has been treated less favourably than a man the sense of the section is that you must compare like with like, and you cannot. When she is pregnant a woman is no longer just a woman. She is a woman, as the Authorised Version accurately puts in, with child, and there is no masculine equivalent."

It is interesting to note that this case was decided by majority only. The dissenting judgment did not accept that a woman dismissed from her employment on the ground of pregnancy has no protection under the Act because such a "bald assertion seems to contradict both the spirit and the letter of the statutes". As regards the finding a comparison, it was argued that a pregnant woman should be compared to a "sick" man because both will require time off for medical reasons. "An employer should not discriminate by applying different and less favourable criteria to the pregnant woman than to the man requiring time off."

In light of the subsequent case law in this area, Turley is a curious judgment and would appear to defeat the whole purpose of sex discrimination law. When is a woman more woman than when pregnant? Although Turley has long since been superseded, it is an important judgment if only to appreciate how pregnancy, in terms of sex discrimination, as a subject, has conceptually troubled the courts.

Following on from Turley was the case of Hayes v Malleable Working Man's Club and Institute; Maugham v North East London Magistrate's Court Committee. The Employment Appeal Tribunal in this case overturned the decision of the Industrial Tribunal in Turley. The EAT stated that there was no principle of law preventing the application of the SDA 1975 to cases where a woman claims to have been the victim of direct or indirect sex discrimination on grounds associated with or connected with the fact that she is pregnant.

The EAT approved of the dissenting judgment in Turley and Waite J, in his judgment, stated that, "we have not found any difficulty in visualising cases – for example, that of a sick male employee and a pregnant woman employee, where the circumstances, although they could never in strictness be called the same, could nevertheless be properly regarded as lacking any material difference."

Incidentally, in both of these cases the Claimants argued under the auspices of sex discrimination law rather than the law relating to unfair dismissal because in each case, the Claimants had not accrued the necessary continuity of employment to enable them to bring claims for unfair dismissal.

The approach of the English courts in Hayes continued until the landmark European Court of Justice decision of Elisabeth Pacifica Dekker v Stichting Vormingscentrum voor jong Volwassenen (VJV-Centrum) Plus. In this case the court considered the implications of Council Directive No. 76/207 (The Equal Treatment Directive).

The circumstances of the case were that Mrs Dekker applied for the post of instructor at a training centre for young adults run by VJV-Centrum. A short time later she informed the committee dealing with the applications that she was three months pregnant. The committee, as the most suitable candidate for the job, put her forward. She was however subsequently told that she would not be appointed to the position. VJV Centrum gave an explanation for their decision in saying that because Mrs Dekker was already pregnant at the time of her lodging the application for the position, were VJV-

Centrum to employ her, its insurer would not reimburse the daily benefits that they would pay to her during maternity leave.

The court considered Articles 2(1) and 3 (1) of the Equal Treatment Directive. Article 2(1) states that, "…the principle of equal treatment shall mean that there shall be no discrimination whatsoever on grounds of sex either directly or indirectly by reference in particular to marital or family status." Article 3(1) states, "…that there shall be no direct of indirect discrimination on the grounds of sex…" in relation to (inter alia) "…conditions for access to employment…including promotion."

The court in this case adopted a purposive approach to the interpretation of the Directive. It considered whether a refusal to offer employment to a pregnant woman could be regarded as direct discrimination, "on grounds of her sex." The court stated that the answer would depend on whether the fundamental reason for the refusal of employment is one which apples without distinction to workers of either sex, or conversely, whether it applies exclusively to one sex.

The court stated that, "…it should be observed that only women can be refused employment on grounds of pregnancy and such a refusal therefore constitutes direct discrimination on grounds of sex. A refusal of employment on account of the financial consequences of absence due to pregnancy must be regarded as based, essentially, on the fact of pregnancy. Such discrimination cannot be justified on grounds relating to the financial loss which an employer who appointed a pregnant woman would suffer for the duration of her maternity leave."

The court further stated that an employer is in direct contravention of the principle of equal treatment if he refuses to enter into a contract of employment with a female candidate whom he considers to be suitable for the job where such refusal is based on the possible adverse consequences for him of employing a pregnant woman.

This case of Dekker clarified from a European perspective how the Equal Treatment Directive should be interpreted in terms of the treatment of pregnant women, the rationale being that because only a woman can become pregnant, if she suffers discrimination on the grounds of her pregnancy, that will amount to sex discrimination within the meaning of the Directive. It was therefore not necessary to make a comparison thus superseding the previous (United Kingdom) cases discussed of Turley and Hayes.

Although Dekker applied to the situation of where a pregnant woman was employed under an indeterminate contract, the later case of Webb v EMO Air Cargo Ltd involved the situation where a woman was employed specifically as cover for an existing member of staff who had become pregnant and would be absent for maternity leave. Two weeks after Miss Webb commenced work (which required six month's training) she discovered that she was pregnant whereupon she was dismissed on the basis that she would be unavailable as cover from the existing employee who herself would be on maternity leave.

The House of Lords in this case had to consider whether the dismissal had amounted to sex discrimination within the remit of the Sex Discrimination Act 1975. Lord Keith in his judgment made the point that Directive 76/207 would in this case, not have direct effect because the Respondent was not the State or an emanation of the State. However he confirmed that it was for the United Kingdom court to construe domestic legislation to accord with the interpretation of the Directive if that can be done without distorting the meaning of the domestic legislation. Lord Keith considered it necessary to refer to the European Court of justice on whether in the circumstances of the case, Miss Webb's dismissal amounted to sex discrimination.

The European Court of Justice referred to Directive 92/85 (the "Pregnancy Workers Directive") which states in Article 10 that, "member states are to take the necessary measures to prohibit the dismissal of workers...during the period from the beginning of their pregnancy to the end of the maternity period."

The court also referred to the fact that the United Kingdom is a party to the 1989 Convention on the Elimination of All Forms of Discrimination Against Women which prohibits dismissal on the grounds of pregnancy or maternity leave. The Court distinguished between a situation where a woman had been hired as a replacement on a temporary basis and where (as in this case) a woman was hired for an indeterminate period of time albeit to cover, in particular, a specific period. The Court stated, "In circumstances such as those of the applicant, termination of a contract for an indefinite period on grounds of the woman's pregnancy cannot be justified by the fact that she is prevented, on a purely temporary basis, from performing the work for which she has been engaged." Such a dismissal would, in the court's view be incompatible with the Directive.

The case was then referred back to the House of Lords for determination. Lord Keith in light of the decision of the European Court of Justice confirmed that the protection afforded by Community law to a woman during pregnancy and after childbirth cannot be dependent on whether her presence at work during maternity is essential to the proper functioning of the undertaking in which she is employed and that any contrary interpretation would render ineffective the provisions of the Directive.

The different situation of non-renewal of fixed term contracts for reasons of pregnancy was clarified in the case of Caruana v Manchester Airport PLC. The Employment Appeal Tribunal distinguished the view of Lord Keith in Webb in which he had given the example of a woman who had been hired for a fixed term but due to pregnancy would be unable to perform any part of the contract and in such circumstances would be unable to claim that she had been the subject of sex discrimination. Buxton J stated, "since pregnancy was a circumstance relevant to her case… and that circumstance could not be present in the case of a man, she…was the object of unlawful discrimination."

A further case to note in considering the legal rules counteracting adverse treatment of pregnant women is that of O'Neill v Govenors of St Thomas More RCVA School and Bedfordshire County Council. This case involved a teacher of religious education who was, as part of her job, expected to teach the principles of Catholicism. She became pregnant following a relationship with a Catholic priest in the locality. Miss O'Neill's employment was terminated and the Employment Appeal Tribunal had to consider whether the case involved sex discrimination. S6 (2) Sex Discrimination Act 1975 provided that it was "…unlawful for a person…to discriminate against…" a woman, "by dismissing her or subjecting her to any other detriment." Mummery J stated, "The critical question is whether, on objective consideration of all the surrounding circumstances, the dismissal or other treatment complained of.... is on ground of pregnancy. It need not be only on that ground. It need not even be mainly on that ground." So long as causation can be proved, dismissal in such circumstances will amount to sex discrimination.

Due to the fact that pregnant woman must prove a causative link between the dismissal and her pregnancy in order to establish a case for sex discrimination this judgment therefore is important in setting out what must be shown to establish sex discrimination.

Directive 92/85 states as its purpose, "to implement measures to encourage improvements in the safety and health at work of pregnant workers and workers who have recently given birth or who are breastfeeding." As stated previously, Article 10 states that, " Member States shall take the necessary measures to prohibit dismissal of workers, within the meaning of Article 2, during the period from the beginning of their pregnancy to the end of the maternity leave…" Added protection is given in Article 10 (2), which states that an employer must provide written substantiated grounds for dismissing an employee during this period.

Having discussed the protection afforded to women during pregnancy, an important question however relates to the duration of the protection following birth. After what period does the protection cease? In the case of Handels- og Kontorfunktionaerernes Forbund i Danmark v Dansk Arbejdsgiverforening which considered the provisions of Directive 76/207 the court asked the question whether, on the basis that Articles 5(1) and 2(1) encompass dismissal as a consequence of absence due to illness which is attributable to pregnancy or confinement, is the protection against such a dismissal unlimited in time?

The court in this case considered the economic grounds involved and stated that if protection was afforded for an unlimited period of time, this would entail, "not only administrative difficulties and unfair consequences for employers but also negative repercussions on the employment of women."

The court went on to distinguish between the periods prior to and after maternity leave and confirmed that the protection afforded to pregnant women would extend for the duration of the maternity leave but would cease thereafter. The court justified this reasoning by stating that, "In the case of an illness manifesting itself after the maternity leave, there is no reason to distinguish an illness attributable to pregnancy or confinement from any other illness. Such a pathological condition is therefore covered by the general rules applicable in the event of illness." The duration of protection established in this case was upheld in the later case of Handels- og Kontorfunktionaerernes Forbund i Danmark v Dansk Handel and Service in which the court stated "Outside the periods of maternity leave…a woman is not protected against dismissal on the grounds of absence due to an illness originating in pregnancy…"

A further issue of relevance is whether, illness in pregnancy before maternity leave commenced, could be added to post maternity leave absences to determine whether a woman was treated less favourably than a man. The position was clarified in the case of Brown v Rentokil Ltd when the European Court of Justice stated, "where a woman is absent owing to illness resulting from pregnancy or childbirth, and that illness arose during pregnancy and persisted during and after maternity leave, her absence not only during maternity leave but also during the period extending from the start of her pregnancy to the start of her maternity leave cannot be taken into account for computation of the period justifying her dismissal under national law.."

It is clear therefore that the non-discrimination principle affords protection for a woman from the time that she informs her employer of her pregnancy until the time she returns from maternity leave.

A woman is protected from being treated less favourably for bringing proceedings under the EA and a further point to note relates to the shifting of the burden of proof from a woman to her employer. The EA states that where she proves facts from which the tribunal could conclude in the absence of an adequate explanation from her employer that he has committed an act of discrimination, the tribunal shall uphold the complaint unless the employer proves that he did not commit that act. This is an important statutory development to assist a pregnant woman to overcome the hurdle of establishing causation.

Section 99 Employment Rights Act 1996 states that a dismissal is automatically unfair if the principal reason for the dismissal is related to pregnancy. Importantly, there is no minimum period of continuous employment required. The right not to be dismissed by a reason related to pregnancy is essential to counteract adverse treatment of pregnant women in the form of dismissal. However, a major difficulty for a pregnant woman is showing that the principal reason for the dismissal was in fact pregnancy. Should a pregnant employee be dismissed, without specific objective evidence, proving the reason for dismissal can be a major obstacle to overcome in order to establish that she has been unfairly dismissed.

Pursuant to s92 (4) of the Act, a woman who is dismissed during pregnancy or after childbirth is entitled to a written statement setting out the reasons for the dismissal. Such a written statement is admissible as evidence in any proceedings.

In order to counteract adverse treatment for pregnant women, it is essential for legal provisions to ensure that a woman who is on maternity leave receives pay. Otherwise a woman may be subject to adverse financial treatment when she is in a most vulnerable position. The level of pay however is important and the Pregnant Workers Directive states that the level of maternity pay must not be less than the minimum sick pay in the Member State concerned. It must be queried however whether this financial protection is adequate. In analysing the position of a pregnant woman the answer surely is that it is not. A pregnant woman is not entitled to receive her full pay whilst on maternity leave

Every woman is entitled to 26 weeks maternity leave but a woman is only entitled to statutory maternity pay if she has been employed for at least 26 weeks in the 15th week before her baby is due. A woman may be entitled to additional maternity leave of 26 weeks but only if she has, at the beginning of the fourteenth week before the expected week of childbirth, been continuously employed for a period of not less than 26 weeks. In a labour market in which there is a large number of female workers in transient employment this serves only to absent vital protection that should be available without restriction.

It would be unfair if a woman, during maternity leave were not entitled to the benefit of all of her terms and conditions of employment that she would have received had she been working. In the case of Caisse nationale d'assurance viellesse des travailleurs salaries v Evelyne Thibault the European Court of Justice stated, "The principle of non-discrimination requires that a woman who continues to be bound to her employer by her contract of employment during maternity leave should not be deprived of the benefit of working conditions which apply to both men and women and are the result of that employment relationship." As such the Court held that to deprive a woman (due to her absence for maternity leave) of the right to an assessment of her performance and thus depriving her of the possibility of qualifying for promotion was contrary to the Equal Treatment Directive.

In terms of health and safety Article 7 of the Equal Treatment Directive states, "The Directive shall be without prejudice to provisions concerning the protection of women particularly as regards pregnancy and maternity." A question that arises is whether an employer can justify a refusal of access to employment of a pregnant woman on the ground that a prohibition on employment arising on account of the pregnancy would prevent her being employed at the outset and for the duration of the pregnancy in the post of unlimited duration to be filled.

Such a situation arose in Sile-Karin Mahlburg v Land Mecklenberg-Vorpommern in which the court stated that, "...The application of provisions concerning the protection of pregnant women cannot result in unfavourable treatment regarding their access to employment..." The Court concluded that, "Article 2(1) and (3) of the Directive [Equal Treatment Directive] precludes a refusal to appoint a pregnant woman to a post for an indefinite period on the ground that a statutory prohibition on employment attaching to the condition of pregnancy prevents her from being employed in that post from the outset and for the duration of the pregnancy."

This case is an important one in that it removes potential justification for an employer to refuse access to employment to a pregnant woman on the ground of protection under the law. To allow this would have enabled the legal rules for the protection of women to be used to deny access to employment, a situation, which would have brought unfair treatment of pregnant women.

It would be a real burden on women however (as traditionally the primary carers of children) to have to return to work after the birth of a child on the same work terms as prior to the birth. A reduction or variation in the hours worked may be necessary and Part 8A of Employment Rights Act 1996 deals with the issue of flexible working. S80F provides a "qualifying employee with the right to apply to her employer to vary the hours, times and location of her work. However, an employer has nine grounds to justify refusing such an application, to include the burden of additional costs and inability to re-organise work among existing staff giving the employer wide powers to dismiss an application. This constitutes a major limitation of the legislation.

Should a complaint against refusal be upheld, a tribunal can award compensation up to a maximum of eight weeks pay. However, this sum for a woman who may be low paid and perhaps works part time (thus receiving lesser remuneration) will amount to relatively minimal sums in compensation and will not constitute a punitive sanction against an unreasonable employer.

For a pregnant woman it is essential that she and her baby be kept safe and well within the work environment. A pregnant woman is entitled to take paid time off for ante natal care and the law by virtue of the Health and Safety at Work Regulations 1999 states that a risk assessment be undertaken to assess whether the work is of a kind to risk the health and safety of a new or expectant mother or her child. Should the work pose such a risk then an employer shall (if it is reasonable to do so) alter working conditions or hours of work. Should it not be reasonable to do this then a pregnant woman must (where available) be offered alternative work and where this is not possible, the woman must be suspended from work and is entitled to be paid.

Different studies have shown that vague awareness of employment rights at the beginning of pregnancy was found consistently among most women in all groups and that young mothers especially, were less likely to know what their maternity rights were. One suggestion by a women surveyed was that there should be better advertising of pregnancy and maternity rights, "like the tax credit adverts", in order to stimulate public awareness of the rights of pregnant women. Whilst ignorance of the law is no excuse, the law cannot possibly be considered adequate if both the party for whom the law aims to protect and the party on whom there is the obligation to protect are ignorant of its implications or existence. Such lack of awareness and understanding is a further failing of the law in this area and will inevitably lead to unsafe practices and conditions for pregnant women.

Although there is the law relating to risk assessments, attitude of employers is still vitally important. In one study women complained that despite the fact that a risk assessment had been carried out, it had been treated as a mere formality rather than to make sure that the mother and baby were not at risk. The legal rules in isolation therefore, may well prove to be inadequate without an employer embracing the spirit and purpose of the rules also, to prevent unfair and unsafe treatment.

In considering the inadequacy of the law, the effectiveness of the remedy for breach must be assessed. There is a three-month time limit for registering a pregnancy related claim with the employment tribunal. This is in alignment with claims in other areas of employment law. Should the law provide the same time limit for pregnant women as other employees? Although there is provision for extending the time limits this will only be done where the tribunal is convinced that, "it was not reasonably practicable for a complaint to be presented" within the three months.

Pregnancy and the caring for a new baby is without doubt a life changing and potentially stressful event. A new mother (or mother to be) will experience physical, emotional, practical and financial changes. At this time of flux, should there be the same time limit for bringing a claim in the tribunal as is applicable in other circumstances? In the paper "Time to Deliver" it is recommended that the time limit be extended. Women, "cannot face the stress and expense of litigation while still pregnant or caring for a new baby," and it is argued that extending the time limit for bringing a claim would give more women access to justice, "…the option of litigation comes at a time when she has other competing priorities and for women who have no family support or cannot afford legal assistance, legal action may simply not be realistic." Women were also concerned that taking action would harm their current and future job prospects.

Studies suggest that women who work during pregnancy are perceived as less hard working and not worthy of training. Fellow employees sometimes view pregnant workers as less committed, more emotional and irrational. "After I told him (the manager) I was pregnant his whole attitude towards me changed. I couldn't do anything right after that. He made me feel that I'd been letting colleagues down and not pulling my weight, even though I hadn't had much time off except for my appointments."

A further view expressed by women was that their experience of work for during pregnancy and maternity, depending largely on the attitude of other members of staff which was "hit and miss" and did not depend necessarily on the establishment but the individual staff in question. "You could have an excellent manager in one office who was very upfront with equal opportunities, it just depends on each office really. Basically there's nothing wrong with the procedure and policy, its actually the people that are administering it and it depends on the staff, on the senior managers and managers, how they treat you, and how they run the office really."

There appears to be prevailing negative attitudes regarding pregnancy in employment establishments. Hence the law will be unable (and is by itself inadequate) to ensure that a pregnant woman's treatment at work is a positive experience. As it stands, treatment that is clearly unfair may not amount to a breach of the law. An additional reason why the legal rules appear inadequate relates to the proof of discrimination. There is a common view amongst women that even if they suspect discrimination, they will not be able to prove it. The law does not presume discrimination (although as discussed above the burden of proof can be shifted to the employer) and as such women will not bring claims for compensation for fear of being unable to prove that discrimination has occurred. In one focus group the view held was that, "I think they could quite easily give other reasons and they can give you any number of reasons as to why not. It would be very hard to prove that it was actually because you were pregnant I'm sure." The issue of causation is one that causes great difficulty for women and undoubtedly serves to deter otherwise meritorious claims.

As has been discussed above, there is a voluminous patchwork of legal rules relating to the treatment by employers of pregnant women in the workplace. It has been documented, with the assistance of research evidence that although pregnancy should be an exciting and happy experience, in practice, the treatment often received falls very short of this mark. It is clear from considering the law governing the treatment of pregnant women in the workplace that the law has evolved hugely since the days of Turley and Hayes. Great strides, with the influence of Europe, have been made and the influence of social policy can be seen in legal rules today. Pregnant women benefit from greater protection than ever before. So, with such developments, it begs the question as to why so many women report negative experiences in the work place during pregnancy.

It is clear that there is a lack of knowledge and understanding, on the part of employers and employees, of the law. Employers (especially those smaller ones without Human Resources departments) and employees, put simply, do not know the law. As a result, employment policies are not applied properly and women themselves are ignorant of their rights. Consequently, this leads to unfair treatment and as regards (inter alia) health and safety, unsafe and unlawful treatment.

Pregnancy is not a discrete area of the law and there is no applicable code of practice to guide employers and employees through the tangled web that is the law.

From the research evidence, it is very apparent that the law as it stands and by itself, is inadequate to ensure that pregnant women are treated positively and fairly. There must be a shift in attitude for employers. The cost of replacing an employee is estimated at approximately half of their first year salary. Losing staff following pregnancy can be avoided and there is no reason whatsoever why a women cannot return from maternity leave to play an important role for her employers. However the mindset of the employer (and fellow employee) population must change. Employers can recover maternity pay from the state. As such they do not suffer a direct financial loss. Members of staff are absent for different reasons and it is a fact that no place of work can remain static. However without proper understanding and better awareness, pregnant women will continue to suffer at the hands of their employers.

Pregnancy is a natural event. Without it the population would die. The percentage of women who work is increasing. It is surely time therefore for the law to accommodate pregnant women in a positive and proactive way. The law should be comprehensible, accessible and enforceable. Good employers were they familiar with the law would surely wish to comply, whilst those bad employers should be punished for their failures. This would support and serve the cause of women to help ensure that pregnancy is a truly exciting and happy experience.

The EA provides that it is unlawful for an employer to discriminate against a disabled person in relation to such person's employment. The definition of disability discrimination has continuously evolved since the era of Disability Discrimination Act 1995 and implementation of the Equal Treatment Directive in the form of Disability Discrimination Act (Amendment) Regulations 2003.

The EA provides that direct discrimination occurs in circumstances where due to a person's disability, he is treated less favourably than a person not having that particular disability. As with race and sex, there is no defence of objective justification to direct discrimination. In establishing less favourable treatment, the comparator should be a person without the particular disability, whose circumstances are the same as, or not materially different, from the disabled person concerned.

The duty on the part of an employer to make reasonable adjustments, is imposed by virtue of the EA. This duty applies where a provision, criteria or practice applied by or on behalf of an employer, or any physical features of the employer's premises, place a disabled person at a substantial disadvantage compared with non-disabled persons. In Archibald v Fife County Council, the HL held that the duty to make adjustments was triggered when the employee was put at a substantial disadvantage because of a disability, thereby making it impossible to perform the main function of the job. Such employee would be at risk of dismissal – A risk that would not have arisen for a non disabled employee.

The EA provides that disability related discrimination occurs in circumstances where a disabled person is treated less favourably than others, for a reason relating to his disability, and, that the treatment in question cannot shown to be justified. This concept is different to direct discrimination as the comparator is an employee for whom the reason for the treatment does not apply. The reason for the difference in comparators, is that for direct discrimination the comparator is relevant in determining whether or not there is discrimination. However, for disability related discrimination, the comparator is relevant to determining objective justification. In Clark v Novacold, the CA held that the comparison cannot be made until the reason for the treatment is identified. Consequently once a sufficient link has been established between disability and treatment, the focus switches to the issue of justification.

The EA provides that a person has a disability if he has a physical or mental impairment which has a substantial and long term effect adverse effect on his ability to carry out normal day to day activities. The EA also defines that the impairment must have lasted or be likely to last twelve months, or for the rest of the person's life. In establishing a disability, the Tribunal will further consider whether the Claimant suffers from a "clinically well recognised" condition. In determining the same, the Tribunal would consider whether the condition is recognised by WHO, the Disability Code of Practice, and specific declaratory regulations.

In Goodwin v The Patent Office it was held that in order to establish "substantial and long term effect", it was unnecessary for the employee to be completely unable to carry out the activity, but the effect must be more than trivial. However in Morgan v Staffordshire University it was held that the Claimant's "anxiety, stress and depression" was not clinically recognised by WHO and did not establish mental impairment. Similarly, in McNichol v Balfour Beatty Rail Maintenance Ltd the CA declined to confirm an impairment constituting an unspecified back pain, which could not be shown to have been caused by either a clinically recognised physical or mental condition. Nevertheless, in College of Ripon and York St John v Hobbs the EAT held that it was not necessary to establish a clinically recognised psychological illness if the resulting physical symptoms, (progressive muscle wasting and weakness), were in themselves sufficient to fall within the ambit of a "physical impairment".

The EA provides that direct racial discrimination occurs when on racial grounds there is less favourable treatment of a person compared with the treatment of another person. Consequently, an individual will suffer direct racial discrimination where he is treated differently from another because of his racial status. The definition of "racial" is by reference to colour, race, nationality or ethnic or national origins.

In Northern Joint Police Board v Power the applicant claimed that he was rejected for a senior police position in Scotland, because he was English. The EAT held that he was entitled to present a discrimination claim based on his "national origins". Similarly, in Showboat Entertainment Centre v Owens the EAT held that the scope of the RRA 1976 is wide enough to encompass an applicant claiming discrimination based on grounds relating to the race of another person.

The important point is the status of the "comparator", whose circumstances should be materially the same as the applicant, but from a different racial group. In Shamoon v Chief Constable of the RUC the Supreme Court held that the circumstances of the comparator must be the same, or not materially different from that of the applicant. In many circumstances, this may be difficult to achieve. Consequently, where no actual comparator can be found it is permissible to utilise a hypothetical comparator.

In Balamoody v UK Central Council for Nursing the CA held that where there was a prima facie case of discrimination, it would be permissible for the Employment Tribunal to consider how a hypothetical comparator would have been treated, even though the applicant's chosen comparators were inappropriate. It should be noted that the "intention" behind any alleged direct discrimination of the part of X Authority is irrelevant. There is no defence of objective justification to an act of direct discrimination.

James v Eastleigh BC involved the application of the "but for" test to sexual discrimination. In this case, the HL held that even though there was no intention on the part of the local authority to discriminate, the reality was that but for the applicant's sex he was treated less favourably.

Having established an absence of direct racial discrimination, consideration should be given as to whether there is any evidence of indirect discrimination on the part of X Authority. As has already been discussed, this occurs where there is treatment which at first sight appears to be unconnected with racial grounds, religion or belief, but nevertheless such treatment turns out to have a disproportionately adverse impact on members of a particular racial group, religion or belief. In essence, indirect discrimination is the application of an unjustifiable requirement or condition to all persons. This is such that a considerably smaller proportion of persons not of that colour or nationality can comply.

In order to assess whether a considerably smaller proportion of persons within a certain racial group can comply with a requirement or condition, compared to members of other racial groups, a "pool" must be identified for comparison. The "pool" will generally consist of all those to whom the requirement or condition is applied, and will then be divided into members of the Claimant's racial group, and members of other racial groups. In London Underground Ltd v Edwards it was held that the appropriate "pool" will depend on the facts of each case and which section of the public is likely to be affected by the requirement.

In Redfearn v Serco the applicant was dismissed on health and safety grounds for being a member of the BNP. There was a fear for his future safety in view of the multi-racial mix of the workforce. The EAT held that the defence of "health and safety grounds" had been significantly influenced by considerations of race. Consequently, and in defence to a charge of indirect discrimination, it would not be correct to assert that health and safety grounds could be a proportionate means of achieving a legitimate aim.

Chapter 7 – Termination of employment

At common law there are several ways in which an employment relationship can be ended. These include, termination by the employer, (known as dismissal), termination by the employee (known as resignation) and termination by mutual agreement.

Termination of the relationship is initially governed by the terms of the employment contract. However this in itself offers insufficient protection to the employee in circumstances where the employer has unilaterally and unfairly brought the employment to an end. Consequently, both common law and Stautute have evolved in order to regulate not only what rights and remedies are available upon termination, but also, the procedure that should be adopted at the end of the relationship.

A dismissal on the part of the employer can either be express or constructive. Such a constructive dismissal occurs in circumstances where the employee has resigned without notice by reason of the employers conduct. Consequently, the issue has arisen as to what sort of conduct on the part of the employer entitles the employee to immediately resign.

The leading case is that of Western Excavating Ltd v Sharp (1978) QB 761. The employee requested an advance from his employer of accrued holiday pay. This was refused. The employee resigned and claimed that the refusal was so unreasonable so as to amount to a constructive dismissal. Lord Denning MR held that in order to successfully show that a constructive dismissal had occurred, four conditions were necessary;

1. there must be a breach of an express or implied term of the employment contract on the part of the employer.

2. the breach must be repudiatory and be sufficiently important to justify resignation.
3. the employee must have left the employment because of the breach in question
4. the employee should not delay too long.

In the case of Harkulak v Cantor Fitzgerald (2004) IRLR 1942, the employee was subject to foul and abusive language from his employer, which had gone on for a period in excess of six months. This behavior was held to be so unreasonable as to constitute a breach of mutual trust and confidence, entitling the employee to assert constructive dismissal.

Once a dismissal has occurred, it is necessary to establish whether the dismissal is lawful, both at common law and pursuant to statute. At common law, a dismissal can lawfully occur either with notice, or summarily without notice. In order to justify a summary dismissal, the employee must be in breach of an important express or implied term of the contract. If summary dismissal cannot be justified, then the employee has become wrongfully dismissed.

With regard to a lawful dismissal at common law, regard needs to be had to any notice clause contained within the employment contract. In Abrahams v Performing Rights Society (1995) IRLR 486, the employment contract provided for a two year notice period or two years pay in lieu of notice. The employer dismissed the employee without giving any notice, and an issue arose as to whether the employee was under a duty to mitigate his loss. The court held that where the contract itself expressly made provision for payment in lieu, then summary dismissal would be lawful. Consequently, the employee was entitled to treat his payment in lieu not as damages, but as a payment made pursuant to the contract. Therefore, he was under no duty to mitigate his loss, and he would be entitled to two years pay in accordance with his contract.

Compare Cerberus v Powley (2001) IRLR 160, in which the contact specified a six month notice clause. However, payment in lieu was expressed to be discretionary. Consequently, the court held that the employee was under a duty to mitigate his losses on the basis that his claim was for contractual damages.

In order to justify a summary dismissal, there must be a breach of contract on the part of the employee. This breach must be sufficiently serious to enable the employer to summarily dismiss. It can be a breach of either an express or implied term. If the former, then the relevant contractual clause must be carefully defined.

In Dietman v London Borough of Brent (1998) IRLR 299, the employee was summarily dismissed after publication of a Public Report criticising her conduct. The employment contract permitted summary dismissal for gross misconduct and this defined by the contract accordingly. The court held that on a narrow interpretation of the employee's contract, her conduct did not fall within the contractual definition. Hence in this case, she had been wrongfully dismissed.

Once a wrongful dismissal has been established, then at common law the employee is entitled to damages. The aim of such damages is to put the employee in the position he would have been, had the contract been properly performed.

Such damages will include the notice period. In the absence of a contractual notice period then the employee is entitled to statutory notice pay pursuant to the ERA which is one week pays for every year of service up to a maximum of ten weeks pay. The employee would also be entitled to claim damages based on a failure by the employer to follow contractual disciplinary procedures. In Boyo v Lambeth London Borough Council (1994) ICR 527 it was held that the measure of damages would be the loss suffered by the employee as a result of that failure.

Section 94(1) Employment Rights Act 1996 states that every employee has the right not to be unfairly dismissed. If the dismissal is discriminatory, the employee may bring a discrimination claim on the grounds of sex, race, religion or sexual orientation.

An employee who is dismissed by virtue of discrimination or for an inadmissible reason, does not have to show a qualifying period of employment with his employer. However, for other types of unfair dismissal, a qualifying period of two years from the effective date of termination (EDT) is required.

The largest proportion of unfair dismissals, relate to the employer's failure to show one of the five statutory fair reasons for dismissal. They are;
1. capability
2. conduct
3. redundancy
4. statutory illegality
5. some other substantial reason

The date of the EDT is calculated by reference to whether the employee was dismissed with or without notice. If summarily or constructively dismissed, then the EDT starts on the day that the employee left employment. However, if the employee was dismissed on notice, then the EDT does not start to run until the expiry of the notice period.

In determining whether a dismissal was fair for one of the five statutory reasons, the onus is on the employer to show that not only has one of the above reasons has been properly set out, but also that the employer acted reasonably in the circumstances. If the employer fails to show that he acted reasonably with regard to the dismissal, then notwithstanding whether the dismissal falls within one of the five statutory reasons, such dismissal will constitute an unfair dismissal. Such issue of reasonability forms the basis of many cases relating to dismissal.

If an employer claims that an employee was fairly dismissed for capability, then clear evidence will be required in support. Section 98(3) ERA defines capability as 'capability assessed by reference to skill, aptitude, health or any other physical or mental quality'.

In incompetence cases, the Tribunal will not accept a purely subjective assessment. There must be evidence of consultation with the employee, warnings and the giving of an opportunity for the employee to improve.

In Morgan v Electrolux 1991 IRLR 89, the employee was a secretary and was found to have overbooked piece-work. In explaining her activities, she asked to demonstrate her work speed. This request was refused. The Court held that the employers had not acted reasonably in denying her this opportunity.

Nevertheless, a single act of incompetence can constitute a fair dismissal if the nature of the incompetence was gross and overwhelming. In Alidair Ltd v Taylor 1978 ICR 445, the employee was an airline pilot who effected a particularly bad landing. It was held that the nature of the employee's position was such that a single act endangering the aircraft could justify a fair dismissal.

Capability on the grounds of ill-health are treated with a greater degree of caution. Investigation and consultation are of crucial importance. The employer should effect reasonable enquiries about the nature of the illness, investigate the likely length of absence, the impact of absence on his business and whether alternative work is available. Consultation should be effected with the employee, and medical evidence obtained.

In Lynock v Cereal Packaging Ltd (1988) IRLR 510 the employee's attendance record was poor due to ill health. He was provided with appropriate verbal and written warnings by his employers. The employee was consequently dismissed. The EAT held that this was a fair dismissal taking into account the employee's attendance at work had been poor and intermittent. The employer had gone through the relevant warnings procedures and had carried out their investigations as to the employee's periods of absence in a proper manner.

Where the employer seeks to justify a dismissal on the basis of conduct, then in order to constitute a fair reason, the misconduct must in some way reflect on the employment relationship. Dismissal for misconduct may be appropriate after a series of incidents, or in serious cases of gross misconduct after a single incident.

In Mathewson v RB Wilson Dental Laboratory Ltd 1988 IRLR 512 a senior employee was arrested for possession of cannabis during his lunch break. He was summarily dismissed on returning to work. The dismissal was found to be fair taking into account, the use of prohibited drugs, the involvement of the Police, influence on other members of staff and the suitability of continuing to employ the employee in this particular senior position

The difference between capability and conduct is essentially that capability implies something about the employee's inherent inability to carry out performance of his work under the contract. This can either be due to ill health, incompetence or qualifications. However, conduct requires some positive action on the part of the employee which renders his performance as constituting a breach of the contract and can include disobedience of lawful orders, theft, fraud, taking bribes, persistent lateness and taking unauthorised and prolonged leave.

The five statutory reasons are effectively 'gateways' through which the employer has to pass in order to demonstrate the fairness of dismissal. As previously indicated, the next stage is one of fairness, and is essentially procedural. Section 98(4) ERA provides that the question of whether a dismissal is fair or unfair having regard to the reasons shown by the employer, 'depends on whether in the circumstances the employer acted reasonably or unreasonable in treating it as a sufficient reason for dismissing the employee'.

Consequently, the employer will need to show whether in dismissing his employee, the employer utilised a fair procedure, and, whether the employers decision to dismiss fell within the range of reasonable responses open to a reasonable employer.

In determining whether a fair procedure has been adopted on the part of the employer, regard should be had to the ACAS guidelines and any contractual procedures contained within the employment contract.

In misconduct cases, it would be reasonable for the employer to undertake a proper investigation in establishing the relevant facts of the case. In British Home Stores v Burchell (1978) IRLR 379 the employee was summarily dismissed for theft. The court held that it was not necessary to prove at the time of dismissal that the employee was guilty of theft beyond reasonable doubt. Neither was it necessary for the employer to await the outcome of any criminal conviction. The court held that an employer would be entitled to dismiss if he had actual belief in the employee's guilt, his belief was based on reasonable grounds, and that a proper and reasonable course of investigation was undertaken prior to dismissal.

Nevertheless, only after the employer has undertaken a proper investigation procedure, should he consider activating the dismissal process. The ACAS Code recommends that minor cases of misconduct and poor performance should warrant informal advice, coaching and counselling. If necessary, an informal oral warning should be issued together with a discussion of how the employee needs to improve. The employer should only consider summary action in circumstances involving blatant gross misconduct.

Dismissal must be within the range of reasonable responses which a reasonable employer might make. The Tribunal should not substitute its own view for that of the employer; ie, It should not ask itself whether a lesser penalty would have been reasonable, but rather whether or not dismissal was reasonable. In addition, any investigation carried out by the employer into an employee's alleged misconduct, should fall within the same range of reasonable responses as in relation to the dismissal itself.

In the case of British Leyland UK Ltd v Swift (1981) IRLR 91 the issue arose as to the nature of test to be applied as to what constituted an appropriate band of reasonable responses. Denning MR stated that the basic question to be put should be, 'was it reasonable for the employer to dismiss?' If a reasonable employer would not have dismissed in such circumstances, then the dismissal was unfair. However if a reasonable employer in the same set of circumstances would have dismissed, then the dismissal would be fair. Denning MR referred to a band of reasonability and went onto state that there is "a band of reasonableness, within which one employer might reasonably take one view; another quite reasonably take a different view. Both views might be quite reasonable'.

The band of reasonable responses test has been subsequently criticized. In Haddon v Van Den Bergh Foods Ltd (1999) IRLR 672, the EAT took the view that the test was an unjustifiable extension on the basic test of fairness specified in Section 98(4) ERA.

Nevertheless, in Post Office v Foley; HSBC Bank Plc v Madden (2000) IRLR 827 the Court of Appeal affirmed that the band of reasonable responses test was still appropriate. Mummery LJ took the view that the test should remain binding until "such time as Parliament chose to change the basic statutory text underpinning the test".

A fair dismissal for redundancy must meet with specified criteria in order to constitute a fair dismissal. The employer has a duty to examine the needs of his business and examine any alternatives to redundancy.

The employer must adopt fair criteria in determining selection for redundancy. An example of this is the established practice of "last in first out" (LIFO), although in itself, this is not conclusive in order to establish reasonability on the part of the employer. Other selection criteria can be adopted based on capability. However, it is of crucial importance that any adopted criteria must not be subjective to the employer.

In Williams v Compair Maxim Ltd 1982 IRLR 83 the EAT stated that the employer must act reasonably in treating redundancy as a sufficient reason for the dismissal. The onus was on the employer to carefully manage the redundancy situation, and in so doing regard should be had to the following factors;

1. Warn and consult with affected employees
2. Consult with any relevant Trade Union
3. Adopt a fair selection criteria
4. Apply the selection criteria in a fair and objective manner
5. Effect reasonable efforts to ascertain whether there is any alternative employment

Whenever 20 or more employees are to be made collectively redundant, the employer is required to consult with trade union or employee representatives. This duty of consultation stems from the provisions of Sections 188-198 Trade Union and Labour Relations (Consolidation) Act 1992. The duty arises when an employer is proposing to dismiss twenty or more employees at one establishment within a period of ninety days or less. Section 188 (2) provides that such consultation shall include consultation about the following matters;

1. How the dismissals can be avoided
2. How to reduce the number of employees proposing to be dismissed
3. Mitigation of the consequences of dismissal.

In Middlesborough Borough Council v TGWU (2002) IRLR 332, the employers did not properly consult about all three elements under Section 188 (2); ie, how to avoid the dismissals. Consequently, there was held to be a breach of Section 188.

Redundancy in the context of the Trade Union and Labour Relations Act 1992 (TULRA), includes dismissal for any reason not related to the individual's concern, such as re-organisation, harmonising terms and conditions, as apposed to dismissals for redundancy in the normal sense.

Consultation must begin in good time and in any event, at least ninety days before the first dismissals take effect.

The relevant sections in TULRCA 1992, are intended to implement EU Collective Redundancies Directive 98/59/EC on the issue. However, the Directive does not define the actual event of redundancy. In Junk v Kuhnel (2005) IRLR 310, the ECJ held that 'redundancy' meant the declaration by the employer of his intention to terminate the contract of employment. Therefore, this Case is authority for the proposition that consultation must take place before the notice of dismissal is given, rather than between notice of dismissal and the actual termination of the contract.

Consultation is supposed to be with a view to reach an agreement. This effectively means negotiation, and pursuant to the Junk decision (ante) it is strongly arguable that there is now a duty on the part of the employer to negotiate. Nevertheless, there are limitations on the duty of consultation. In Securicor v GMB (2004) IRLR 9 the employers were proposing to effect collective redundancies although they did not consult on the economic background to the redundancies. The EAT held that there was no duty on the part of the employer to consult on the economic decision forming the background to a redundancy, such as the decision to close specific branches.

If a claim has been presented to ET that the employer has not consulted as required, the Tribunal has a mandatory duty under section 189 (2) to make a declaration to that effect. It has a discretion to make a protective award for a period of up to ninety days.

It is arguable that this sanction is inadequate, as even if the employer fails to negotiate, the remedy is still only a protective award up to a defined maximum period. The tribunal cannot force the employer to reemploy. Once the employer has made up his mind to effect a collective redundancy, then the statutory consultation process is merely a step that is undertaken on the way to eventual dismissal.

It is arguable that the Junk case has modified its position somewhat in that there now appears to be a duty on the part of the employer to negotiate. Even so, the sanction for breach remains the same.

In Radin v GMV (2004) IRLR 400 there was a breach of the Section 188 procedure. The employer put forward a defence that the consultation would have been futile in any event. It was held that the protective award under Section 189 (3) was not a compensatory award, and consequently was not related to the employees losses. The award was in the nature of a 'penal' award, and consequently the employer was under an obligation to discharge the same.

The employers duty to consult on a transfer of business undertaking is similar to that on collective redundancies. The EU Business Transfers Directive has been implemented by the Transfer of Undertakings (Protection of Employment) Regulations 1981.

The employer of any affected employees must inform and consult either with the Trade Union, or if there is none, with appropriate employee representatives. The employer must deliver or post the following information long enough before the transfer occurs to enable consultation to take place;

1. The fact of the transfer, its approximate date and the reasons for it
2. The legal, economic and social implications of the transfer for the effective employees
3. Whether the employer envisages taking matters in relation to the effected employees.

As with collective redundancies, the sanction for inadequate consultation is the issue of a protective award by the employment tribunal. The award cannot exceed ninety days pay.

The Information and Consultation of Employees Regulations 2004 (ICE Regulations) were implemented in order to enforce the EU Directive on information and consultation in the workplace. The ICE regulations currently apply to undertakings with 150 or more employees. These regulations provide a mechanism for employment of worker representatives to negotiate with employers on behalf of employees as an alternative to Trade Union representation.

Except in unionised workplaces, there will usually be no mechanisms for information on consultation to take place. The ICE Regulations enable negotiations to set up an appropriate agreement, either by way of the employer voluntarily starting negotiations, or at least of 10% of employees voting in a written request for an ICE agreement. In the latter case, the employer must start negotiations within three months with negotiating representatives. When there is no approved pre-existing agreement, a new one must be negotiated. The negotiated agreement should set out the circumstances in which employers will inform and consult their employees. The subject matter, method, frequency and timing of information and consultation should also be agreed.

Breach of the ICE Regulations on the part of the employer, will enable a complaint to be presented to the Central Arbitration Committee. The CAC can make an order requiring the employer to take specified steps within a specific period. The relevant applicant may then apply to the EAT for a penalty notice. It is submitted that once again the sanction is inappropriate for breach of this regulation. In a large undertaking, an employer may consider that this is a small price to pay for going ahead with a commercial decision whether or not the ICE regulations are complied with.

Nevertheless, the ICE Regulations represent a culture change in the UK, where traditionally worker representation is carried out through Trade Union representatives. However, there is a risk that the ICE regulations may undermine trade unions in unionised workplaces, by setting up alternative structures. It is also noted that ICE representatives may not have the same experience or negotiating skills as established Trade Union representatives.

There are situations where the employer has a good and fair reason for dismissal, but the dismissal nevertheless turns out to be unfair due to a procedural defect in the manner of dismissal.

The original test was that adopted in British Labour Pump v Byrne 1979 IRLR 94. It was held that where the employer had not followed the correct procedural steps on a conduct dismissal, such action could still be fair if the employer could show that the dismissal would have been reasonable in any event.

In the case of Polkey v A.E. Dayton Services Ltd (1988) AC 344 the employee was was made redundant. He complained that he had been unfairly dismissed because of a lack of consultation. The House of Lords held that the correct approach should be that a tribunal would be entitled to reduce any compensatory award to reflect the likelihood that the employee would have been dismissed in any event. If the tribunal was unable to say with certainty what the outcome of a fair procedure would have been, it had to assess the chances that the employee would have stayed in employment and make a percentage reduction from damages accordingly. It would be up to the employer to show that the employee would have been dismissed in any event. This reduction from damages was known as a 'Polkey reduction'.

There is no doubt that the importance of procedure. Certainly, the employer can no longer terminate the employment without reference to the same. Failure to consult, and comply with a minimum procedure will attract a sanction.

Chapter 8 – Evolution of the employment tribunal system

The concept of a tribunal acting as an alternative mechanism for the resolution of disputes has an established history. There has been a long tradition of administrative tribunals, as a forum of dealing with decisions of the Executive arm of government. However, as the 1954 "Crichel Down" scandal revealed, these administrative tribunals were open to Ministerial abuse.

In 1957 the Franks Committee was set up in response to criticism of the present structure. Franks conceded that there was a problem with the perception of independence. Nevertheless, Franks noted that tribunals possessed certain characteristics which often gave them advantages over the courts. These included "cheapness, accessibility, freedom from technicality, expedition and expert knowledge of their particular subject". Although Franks was not concerned with employment relations, it was concerned about ensuring accessibility by aggrieved parties to a dispute resolution system, in circumstances where the formal court structure was not appropriate or desirable.

The government response to Franks, was enactment of the Tribunals and Inquiries Act 1958. This set up a Council on Tribunals whose remit is to achieve a common performance standard for all tribunals and to ensure fair and open procedure. The Council also submits an annual report on tribunals to the Lord Chancellors Department. Nevertheless, the Council's Statutory powers are limited and this was so particularly with regard to enforcement of its recommendations.

It is submitted that Franks was a turning point in the perception of tribunals. Whereas they had previously been regarded as an extension of the Executive, Franks placed them firmly on the judicial side.

Industrial tribunals were first established under s12 Industrial Training Act 1964 and their original purpose was to consider appeals by employers against training levies imposed under that Act. Their jurisdiction was extended in 1965 to cover claims in respect of the newly introduced statutory redundancy payments.

In 1968 a Royal Commission under Lord Donovan was set up to examine the present state of industrial relations and existing mechanism for the resolution of industrial and labour disputes. One of the principal recommendations was the establishment of statutory machinery to safeguard employees against unfair dismissal. Coupled with this was a further recommendation to extend the jurisdiction of industrial tribunals in the form of a labour tribunal, to include disputes arising between employers and employees arising out of a contract of employment and/or any statutory claims that they may have against each other .

Therefore, by the time Donovan reported, there was already in place a tradition of being able to deal with dispute resolution in specific areas, by way of a tribunal hearing. However, it was particularly concerned that as far as employment disputes were concerned, there was a "multiplicity of jurisdictions". Donovan noted that redundancy disputes had to be dealt with by the industrial tribunals, whereas employment contract disputes could only be dealt with by either the county courts or High Court.

Donovan was of the opinion that this multiplicity of jurisdictions was apt to "lead to waste, to frustration and to delay" . Thus if an employee wished to claim a redundancy payment but at the same time allege a wrongful dismissal, he would have to go to the industrial tribunal for one part of his claim and the county court for another, regardless of the amount in dispute.

By recommending a new statutory remedy for unfair dismissal, the Donovan Commission foresaw that the mechanism for enforcing this remedy should be by way of the tribunal. However, it went further by recommending that while the jurisdiction of the labour tribunal should be exclusive with regard to the statutory claims for redundancy and unfair dismissal, it should in all other matters arising from the employment relationship, "be at the plaintiff's option whether the proceedings are to be instituted in the labour tribunal or in the ordinary courts".

It is submitted that the ethos of Donovan was to provide rights within the employment relationship in favour of the individual employee. Its recommendation of a right not to be unfairly dismissed is a case in point. However, there is often an in-built inequality in the employment relationship in favour of the employer in terms of enforcement of rights. It would not be unreasonable to expect that an employer would have greater access to the court system than an employee, due to the formality and costs involved.

In recommending the setting up of a labour tribunal, this potential inequality was an issue that Donovan sought to address. It expressed the view that labour tribunals should provide "an easily accessible, speedy, informal and inexpensive procedure for the settlement of disputes".

Implementation of Donovan's recommendation was accorded by virtue of the Industrial Relations Act 1971, with the introduction of protection against unfair dismissal. Jurisdiction over unfair dismissal and redundancy claims was given over to a reconstituted industrial tribunal. Subsequent legislation such as the Employment Tribunals Act 1996, has resulted in an expansion of jurisdiction, which has been progressively extended to include a wide range of employment related matters, discrimination, and health and safety issues. They also have jurisdiction over statutory rights which may be exercised against trade unions in relation to discipline, exclusion or expulsion from membership.

Since the Employment Rights (Dispute Resolution) Act 1998, industrial tribunals are now known as employment tribunals, ("the ET"). As a result of s34 Employment Relations Act 1999, there has been a significant expansion in the jurisdiction of the ET. The maximum compensatory award limit is now £60,600. A claim for discrimination has no maximum limit.

Consequently the volume of applications to the ET has increased. The latest Employment Tribunal Service Annual report has shown there to be a 300% increase in the number of applications to the employment tribunal during the ten year period 1990-2000.

The Donovan model of accessibility, informality and flexibility, represented an ideal. This begs the question of whether such an ideal was ever attainable, or doomed to failure at inception. ETs administer an ever increasing complex system of law, which apart from contractual jurisdiction, is entirely statutory. Any system which failed to fully apply the law in the name of informality, or applied it in an unpredictable way, would soon fall into disrepute. Nevertheless it should be noted that at the time Donovan reported, the amount of employment legislation was considerably less, (and probably less complex), than what existed 25 years later. Hence consideration of the Donovan ideal, should also take into account the existing conditions at the time it was formulated.

As with Franks, the Leggatt Report 2001 undertook a general review of tribunals . Leggatt's terms of reference was to ensure that the delivery of justice through tribunals was timely, proportionate and effected within the framework of a coherent structure. In particular, it was noted that the right to a fair trial stipulated by Art. 6 of the European Convention on Human Rights ("the ECHR"), required a tribunal to be independent, impartial and free from bias.

Employment tribunals were first established by the Industrial Training Act 1964. Since then, the role of the tribunals has dramatically changed and they now have jurisdiction to hear many types of claim, the vast majority of which are cases involving unfair dismissal or redundancy pay. Tribunals perform a judicial function, and are creatures of statute. Unlike the courts, they have no inherent jurisdiction and thus it is necessary if a tribunal is to exercise a particular power, that statute creates the power so wished to be exercised. There is no general power, except that a tribunal is required to give effect to European Union law (doctrine of supremacy of EU Law) and the ECHR rights incorporated by the Human Rights Act 1998.

The tribunal, representatives and witnesses remain seated for the hearing and modes of address are relatively informal: Sir or Madam are acceptable and usual, without being too obsequious; Mr or Ms may be used for representatives, parties and witnesses. On the other hand, for most litigants in person and many lay representatives, tribunals will seem highly formal and legalistic. Evidence is usually given on oath or affirmation, witnesses are cross-examined, legal language is used and legal submissions are made. At times the issues before the tribunal will be complex and involve quite complicated legal analysis. Frequently parties will employ legal professionals who are trained in and used to the greater formality of the courts. All this increases the formality and costs of the proceedings, and sometimes causes delays. In the vast majority of cases the issues are quite simple ones of fact and there is no reason why the tribunal should not be able to adjudicate on these cases without the assistance of detailed rules of evidence and procedure and lawyers.

Tribunals are subject to the overriding objective to deal with cases justly, which includes ensuring the parties are on an equal footing, saving expense, dealing with the case in ways which are proportionate to the complexity or importance of the issues, and ensuring that it is dealt with fairly and expeditiously. They must give effect to this objective when exercising any power or interpreting any provision under the Rules and Regulations.

That means, so far as practicable, ensuring that the parties are on an equal footing; saving expense; dealing with the case in ways which are proportionate to the complexity of the issues; and ensuring that the case is dealt with expeditiously and fairly: This objective is similar, although not identical to that applied in the High Court and county court under the Civil Procedure Rules (CPR). Unlike the Rules the CPR refer to dealing with a case in a way proportionate not just to the complexity of the issues but also to the amount of money involved, the importance of the case and the financial position of each party. The CPR also requires the court to allot to a case 'an appropriate share of the court's resources taking into account the need to allot resources to other cases'. The omission of these provisions may provide a useful indication as to how it is intended that tribunals should approach their task in applying the overriding objective to the conduct of cases before them.

Employment tribunals form part of the Employment Tribunal Service, ("the ETS"). The ETS has responsibility for both ET and EAT. In 1997, the ETS was established as an executive agency of the Department of Trade and Industry. However, the connection between the ETS and the DTI led to a perception of lack of independence, particularly in matters which involved the DTI as a party to the dispute.

In his Report, Leggatt noted that there was "an uneasy relationship between most tribunals and the departments on whose decisions they are adjudicating. In those tribunals which are paid for by the sponsoring departments, the chairman and members feel that they cannot be independent, however impartial they are. Indeed, plainly they are not independent".

The engagement of Art. 6 ECHR in relation to links between lay members of the ET and the DTI, came under scrutiny in Scanfuture UK Ltd v Secretary of State for Trade and Industry . Here, the EAT held that "the fair minded and informed observer would have harboured an objectively justified fear that the ET lacked the independence and impartiality required for compliance with Art. 6".

Leggatt recommended that the administrative control of employment tribunals should be transferred from the DTI to the Lord Chancellor's Department and called for the establishment of an independent tribunal service which would be free from executive influence.

Leggatt additionally suggested that rules of procedure for existing tribunals should be updated in order to bring them into line with the civil justice reforms . This would include a more interventialist approach with the adoption of case management procedures in order to ensure that issues could be identified, and weak cases eradicated at an early stage .

In response to Leggatt, the Lord Chancellor announced the introduction of a new, unified Tribunals Service. This agency is an executive department within the Department for Constitutional Affairs, ("the DCA"), and provides common administrative support to the main central government tribunals. During 2006, responsibility for administration of the ETS was taken away from the DTI, and handed over to the Tribunals Service.

The 1997 Labour government had become increasingly concerned at the rising number and cost of employment disputes. The DTI was particularly interested in effecting reforms to encourage and promote workplace conciliation as an alternative to employment tribunal proceedings. In addition, there was a general judicial consensus that rules of procedure should be brought up to date.

During 1998, a report under the chairmanship of Lord Woolf recommended wholesale reform of the rules of civil procedure in the county courts and High Court, culminating in the CPR 1999. These rules of practice radically changed court procedure, with an emphasis on case management, full disclosure and early dispute settlement through the adoption of pre-issue protocols.

At the same time as Leggatt, a separate review on the structure and constitution of employment tribunals, was undertaken by the Employment Tribunal System Taskforce 2002, ("the ETST"), under the chairmanship of Janet Gaymer . The remit of the ETST was to make recommendations as to how the ET could be made more efficient and cost effective against a background of rising tribunal applications.

The ETST had the benefit of reviewing Leggatt, and noted that as employment tribunals were party and party tribunals, they constituted a special case which deserved to be dealt with differently from all other administrative tribunals. In her foreword to the Report, Janet Gaymer stated that the ETST's recommendations were intended to be a coherent strategy for the future development of the ET system. She identified four general principles upon which such recommendations would be based;

    1. Greater co-ordination and consistency of practice in which a proposed co-ordinating body would play a central role.

    2. A shift in the axis of the employment tribunal system so that the emphasis would be on early disclosure of information with a view to identifying the issues in disputes and their efficient resolution.

    3. An emphasis on preventive work and the identification of, and learning from, best practice.

    4. The use of tribunal proceedings as a last resort after all other alternative routes for the resolution of disputes have been exhausted.

Consequently, the ETST recommended the adoption of "in-house" resolution procedures, mediation and alternative dispute resolution as an alternative to employment tribunal proceedings .

With regard to employment tribunal procedure, the ETST recommended standardisation of the method of presenting a claim , the adoption of early disclosure and a procedural timetable and increased use of costs orders in limited situations. It also emphasised the need for a more interventialist approach to case management. The procedural aspects of these recommendations appear to mirror the Civil Procedure Rules in several aspects.

The trio of reports was completed by the Cabinet Office Better Regulation Taskforce 2002, ("the COBRT"), under the chairmanship of David Arculus . The COBRT recommended that the DTI review the impact of employment legislation on businesses, whether such legislation achieved its objectives, the costs of compliance and the impact of employment tribunal cases.

In response to the recommendations of the ETST and COBRT, the government introduced Statutory dispute resolution procedures, aimed at resolving employment disputes without recourse to employment tribunal proceedings. The procedures and related rules were set out in the Employment Act 2002 and the Employment Act 2002 (Dispute Resolution) Regulations 2004. The Statutory dispute resolution procedures attracted significant criticism. As a result of the Employment Act 2008, the EA 2002 has been repealed and the former resolution procedure regime has been abolished.

Chapter 9 – Composition of employment tribunals

Employment Tribunals face an increasing caseload. With the introduction of new employment and discrimination legislation, their jurisdiction has widened. Cases have become more complex, and public awareness of employment rights and recourse to litigation have all contributed to increased pressure on the current system.

Section 21(1) Employment Tribunals Act, provides a jurisdictional list. The ETS website provides a more detailed list by way of clarification . It is immediately apparent that access to the ET is dependent upon a Statutory gateway, and there is no common law right to commence proceedings in the ET.

This limitation on access is understandable if one takes into account the nature of the potential claim and the remedy being sought. Hence a claim for unfair dismissal or redundancy is incapable of being brought in the county court, as pursuant to the ERA 1996, the ET has exclusive jurisdiction, and the civil courts are unable to offer a remedy.

A claim arising out of discrimination is again dependent upon the provision of a Statutory remedy. The common law does not protect against discrimination per se. Accordingly, under the Equality Act 2010, individuals may present a complaint to the ET in respect of that part of the legislation relating to employment. Non-employment matters will require determination by the civil courts, in circumstances where permitted by the enabling legislation.

As previously indicated, Donovan was concerned as to a multiplicity of jurisdictions. He recommended that the jurisdiction of labour tribunals should encompass all disputes arising between employers and employees arising out of their contracts of employment. Unfortunately, there has only been partial implementation of this particular recommendation.

Tribunals can hear claims brought by employees for damages for breach of contract or any sum due under a contract of employment or any other contract connected with employment including settlement agreements concluded before termination of employment: Rock-It Cargo Ltd v Green. The tribunal's jurisdiction is limited, however, to claims which either arise on termination of the contract of employment or which are outstanding on its termination. Tribunals have no jurisdiction to hear a breach of contract claim in respect of compromise agreements not finalised until after termination even if the claim arose because of the termination: Miller Bros and F P Bulter Ltd v Johnston. Likewise, tribunals have no jurisdiction to hear a breach of contract claim that was commenced before the termination: Capek v Lincolnshire County Council.

Section 3(2) Employment Tribunal Act 1996 provides that the ET has jurisdiction for a claim for damages for breach of contract. Consequently it is possible to present a claim for both unfair dismissal and wrongful dismissal before the ET. However, the amount of damages recoverable in the ET for breach of contract is presently £25000. Although it is possible to claim contractual damages at the ET, there is a cap on the amount that can be recovered.

In Fraser v Hlmad Ltd the Claimant brought a breach of contract claim in both the ET and the High Court. He succeeded in recovering £25000 in the ET and then sought to recover the shortfall excess of £55000 in the High Court. The Court of Appeal ("the CA") held that a wrongful dismissal claim could not be split into two separate actions. The cause of action for wrongful dismissal litigated in the ET was the subject of a final judgment and thereafter ceased to exist. Nevertheless, Mummery LJ was critical of the £25000 ET cap, and suggested reconsideration of the jurisdictional limit.

It is submitted that £25000 ceiling is a serious constraint on the ET's contractual jurisdiction. As a result, a potential litigant may still have to consider bringing two separate actions – one for unfair dismissal in the ET, and another for wrongful dismissal in the civil court. In addition, the ET's remedy for a breach of contract is limited to damages and it is unable to offer injunctive relief.

An employee being bullied at work now has a choice. If such employee falls within the discriminatory framework of sex, race, age or disability, then a claim can be presented for harassment arising out of discrimination in the ET. Alternatively, the same employee can issue in the county court pursuant to the PHA. Only one jurisdiction can be used, for as was seen in Fraser v Hlmad Ltd, the doctrine of issue estoppel will apply if the same claim is presented in both jurisdictions.

There are advantages and disadvantages of each jurisdiction. Primary limitation under the PHA is six years, whereas ET has a much shorter limitation period. In the county court, once vicarious liability is established, then the liability of the employer is strict. Conversely, the ET must go through the two stage process set out in Igen Ltd v Wong in order to establish direct discrimination on the part of the employer. The county court will usually award costs in favour of a successful Claimant, whereas in the ET they are not recoverable.

A further major limitation on access to the ET, is in respect of whether a potential litigant falls within the definition of a potential Claimant for the purposes of the legislation. Section 230 ERA 1996 makes a distinction between an employee and a worker. Under s94 ERA 1996, only an employee has the right to present a claim for unfair dismissal. Therefore, if a litigant does not fall within the Statutory definition of an employee, there is no claim for unfair dismissal, and the ET will accordingly decline jurisdiction.

On the other hand, other legislation such as the Working Time Regulations 1998, Part-Time Workers (Prevention of Less Favourable Treatment) Regulations 2000 and the National Minimum Wage Act 1998, all give rights to workers. This definition covers a wider range of people than employees, and can include anyone who has entered into a contract of employment or any other contract to perform personally any work or services.

Hence in many cases the gateway for ET jurisdiction is dependent upon the status of the applicant, and whether such person falls within the Statutory definition of the legislation under which a remedy is being sought. In Redrow Homes (Yorkshire) Ltd v Wright a group of sub-contractors was classified as workers for the purposes of the Working Time Regulations. Conversely in Lawson, Pardoe & Del Fabro the CA held that a pupil barrister was not a worker for the purposes of the National Minimum Wage Act.

The ETS provides administrative support to both employment tribunals and employment appeal tribunals. Its principal activities include dealing with all administration and correspondence relating to tribunal cases, making practical arrangements for tribunal hearings and providing information on tribunal procedures to the public.

The number of employment tribunal offices within the UK, is far removed from that originally envisaged by Donovan. He postulated that, "industrial tribunals will be operating in all major industrial centres and thus easily accessible". However, that assumption never became a reality. Since 1971 there has been a decline in the number of hearing centres, which is entirely due to the issue of resources.

The ET panel, is tripartite in its composition and consists of a legally qualified employment judge and two lay members. With the objective of ensuring balance, reg 8 ETR provides that selection of ET members is made from three panels, one member from each. Each lay member is drawn from separate panels of employee and employer representatives appointed by the Secretary of State. ET judges consist of barristers and solicitors of at least seven years standing. Selection of the other two persons from each of the other panels is made after consultation with employer and employee organisations.

It is simplistic to assume that one panel recommends the appointment of lay members from the trade union movement, and the other panel from members of the CBI. Lay members come from many different backgrounds, and many lay members are not members of a union or the CBI. Competition for appointment as a lay member is fierce, and the Employment Tribunal Members Association takes an active part in the appointment process.

It is now possible for individuals to apply direct to the DCA for lay membership of the ET. Membership of a sponsoring employer or employee organisation, is no longer a pre-requisite for appointment. This is a similar approach to that taken for the appointment of lay magistrates, and reflects the declining influence and membership of sponsor bodies such as the trade union movement.

As with lay magistrates, lay members of the ET are subject to an ongoing competency framework, and have to undergo a re-appointment process. However, there is an established perception of the majority of lay magistrates being middle aged and having a middle-class background. Although some ET lay members are also lay magistrates, it is submitted that the panel selection criteria for the ET does ensure a more diverse socio-economic lay membership.

Lay members can participate fully at an ET hearing. This can include asking direct questions of a witness. In arriving at a decision, all three members have an equal vote and it is not unknown for the chairman to be outvoted by the two lay members. Although the ET judge's principal purpose is to advise his co-members on matters of law, all three members participate in findings of fact. This is quite different to the magistrates court, where lay magistrates will never sit with a district judge. Indeed, the only time lay magistrates sit with a professional judge, is on appeal at the Crown Court.

The EAT is also tripartite in composition. The legally qualified chairman is always an appropriately certified High Court or county court judge. However, the two lay members usually have several years experience as ET lay members, and it is not unusual to find a lay EAT member who has achieved some recognition in public life. There is no evidence to suggest that the balance of power in the EAT between lay members and the chairman, is different to that of the ET.

There is a growing perception that Employment judges tend to favour legally qualified advocates, in preference to lay representation. It is tempting to dismiss out of hand this observation in the absence of satisfactory statistical evidence in support. In Chris Project v Hutt an Employment judge at the outset of a case and on review of documentation, said to the employer's representative, (who was not a legal representative), that there may be some difficulty in establishing that the claimant was unfairly dismissed. The EAT noted that the representative was "anxious, not confident and it was easy to envisage that he would have been vulnerable to pressure". Consequently, the EAT held that there was an appearance of bias and set aside the original ET judgment.

There is now an increase in the number of occasions when Employment judges are allowed to sit alone, and therefore the issue of potential bias, is an important one. The Employment judge's power to sit alone is usually exercised in interim applications to the ET as part of its case management function and at pre-hearing review. The judge will frequently effect interim orders, such as disclosure of documentation or exchange of witness statements either at a case management discussion, or pre-hearing review. Very often, an interim order is made in the absence of the parties, or on a written application by either of them.

In Sutcliffe v Big C's Marine the Employment judge decided that there should be a pre-hearing review in order to determine which of three companies was the correct employer for the purposes of the claim. The judge's decision to hear the matter alone was criticised by the EAT, on the basis that that this was an issue of fact which required determination before a full tribunal.

The practice of allowing an Employment judge to sit alone, certainly saves time and valuable ET recourses. It would be an unnecessary expense to require a full panel to hear all interim applications as well as delaying the whole claims process.

The Employment Tribunal Rules of Procedure provide that a hearing is held for the purpose of determining outstanding procedural or substantive issues, or disposal of the proceedings. The hearing must be held in public and usually before a chairman and two lay members. The ET is specifically required to avoid formality as far as is appropriate and is not bound by the strict rules of evidence applied in the civil courts. Hence hearsay evidence is admissible.

It is right that as a tribunal, the ET should take a less formal approach to the admissibility of evidence. Nevertheless, the ET remains an adversarial forum, and it will not determine on an evidential point that has been omitted by either party. Hence in Derby County Council v Marshall an unrepresented Respondent failed to establish a fair reason for dismissing the Claimant. The EAT held that there was no obligation on the part of the ET to investigate whether there was any fair reason which the Respondent could have relied upon.

In addition, although the rules of evidence may be relaxed, it is submitted that rules of procedure are not. The procedural hurdles which must be overcome in order to bring a claim to a hearing are complex and more suited a civil court rather than a tribunal. Drafting and exchange of witness statements, submission of a schedule of loss, and the compilation of a bundle of documents, are not matters that can be easily dealt with by the average litigant in person.

Each party to the dispute may give evidence, call and question witnesses. The fact that Legal Aid is not available in England & Wales means that a significant proportion of litigants are unrepresented. There is anecdotal evidence to show that where employers are legally represented and applicants are not, the success rate of the latter is lower than where both have legal representation.

The ET has the power to award compensation, reinstatement or re-engagement. Alternatively, the tribunal can make a finding on liability and order a separate remedies hearing. This may be the case if the Respondent is seeking to argue a reduction in the compensatory element of the award pursuant to the principle of Polkey v AE Dayton Services Ltd .

In a complex case or where time has run out, judgment may be reserved. However, it has been argued that the handing down of a reserved judgment may constitute a breach of Art. 6 ECHR, which requires a fair hearing to be conducted in a reasonable time. In Bangs v Connex South Eastern Ltd a delay of twelve months rendered the judgment unsafe and required the case to be remitted for rehearing.

There are limited circumstances in which the ET is able to effect a costs order. Unlike the civil courts, an adverse costs order is not normally awarded, even if the Respondent is successful. As a consequence, it is possible that commercial pressure alone results in some employers settling unmeritorious claims. However opportunistic litigation also occurs in the civil courts and is not confined solely to the ET. On the other hand, it is arguable that the limited circumstances in which costs can be awarded acts as a deterrent to the pursuing of an ET claim. There is also anecdotal evidence to show that the recent introduction of ET fees on issue of proceedings has had an adverse effect on the number of presented claims. An employee without access to funding, legal expense insurance or trade union support will have difficulty in securing legal representation.

The ETR distinguish between a paying party and a receiving party. The former identifies the party against whom an adverse costs order has been made, and the latter, the beneficiary of the order. If the receiving party is legally represented, then a costs order will be made. However if the receiving party is not represented, then the ET is able to effect a preparation time order. A preparation time order is an innovation introduced by the ETR. The ET cannot make both a costs order and a preparation time order in favour of the same receiving party.

The ET is empowered to make a costs order, where in bringing or conducting the proceedings the paying party or its representative, has acted vexatiously, abusively, disruptively or otherwise unreasonably, or the bringing or conducting of the proceedings by the paying party has been misconceived. The ET is also able to effect an order for costs where the failure of the paying party has resulted in an adjournment of a hearing, or, the paying party has not complied with an order or practice direction made by the tribunal. Similar provisions apply to the making of a preparation time order.

As a result of the ETR there is now a greater risk than before of costs being awarded against the defaulting party. It is arguable that this acts as a deterrent on the part of the employee, although this can be a two edged sword. In McPherson v BNP Paribas the EAT held that in deciding to award costs, the overriding issue was not whether the claim itself was unreasonable, but whether the paying party conducted proceedings unreasonably.

In Lodwick v L.B. Southwark the CA affirmed that costs awards remain exceptional and should not be the norm in ET proceedings. Hence, so long as both parties properly run their respective cases, and the claim or defence is not unreasonable and not misconceived, there is no reason to expect an adverse costs order being made.

Consequently, a costs order may be considered an appropriate sanction where the defaulting party's behaviour, was in contravention of the ETR. In Sutton v The Ranch Ltd the Respondent failed to enter a Response giving rise to a default judgment. The EAT refused costs, on the basis that there is no obligation to enter a Response. However, in BSM v Fowler the Respondent failed to lodge a timely Response, and then applied to set aside the default judgment with leave to defend. Here, the EAT upheld an adverse costs order against the Respondent.

It can be viewed that costs sanctions are a potential method of dealing with weak and vexatious cases. Weak and vexatious cases can undermine the credibility of the whole ET system. An increase in the power of the ET to make costs orders may result in increased legal representation. Just as the possibility of an adverse costs order can act as a deterrent, so the prospect of potential costs recovery may encourage legal participation. It can also be viewed that there is a correlation between legal representatives and the level of financial compensation achieved for their clients, as they possess special characteristics not shared by other representatives. They are more suited to the adversarial nature of the ET, due to their training, strategic capability and better presentation of evidence.

Chapter 10 – Settlement agreements

A Settlement agreement, (formerly known as a "Compromise agreement"), is a legally binding agreement for settlement of a statutory employment claim. These agreements are the principal mechanism for settling statutory employment claims and the necessary requirements are set out in s203(3) ERA 1996;

1. The Settlement agreement must be in writing.
2. The Settlement agreement must relate to the particular complaint.
3. The employee or worker must have received independent legal advice from a qualified adviser as to the terms and effect of the Settlement agreement. In particular, its effect on the ability to pursue rights before an ET.
4. At the time the adviser gives advice, a policy of insurance covering the risk of a claim by the employee or worker for inappropriate advice.
5. The Settlement agreement must identify the adviser.
6. The agreement must state that the statutory conditions regulating Settlement agreements are satisfied.

The requirements under s203(3) ERA are applied strictly. A Settlement agreement which fails to comply with the statutory regime will not be valid. The effect of a valid Settlement agreement is to waive an employee's statutory rights. These rights are different from common law rights, which are capable of being waived.

However an agreement which does not comply with s203(3) ERA does not wholly mean that it is invalid so far as any common law claims are concerned. In Sutherland v Network Appliance Ltd (2000) the parties entered into an agreement which sought to settle both statutory claims and common law claims. It was common ground that the agreement did not comply with s203(3) ERA and therefore did not operate to effectively compromise any of the claimant's statutory claims. However, the agreement also purported to settle the claimant's common law breach of contract claim. The EAT held that to the extent the agreement contained a settlement of contractual claims, it remained enforceable.

It should be noted that a Settlement agreement is not the only mechanism of settling a statutory employment claim. Settlement can be reached through ACAS. The new ACAS Code of Practice on Settlement agreements is relevant.

As an alternative, settlement of a claim at an advanced stage of employment tribunal proceedings can be achieved via a consent order. An employment tribunal will usually be amicable to the granting of a consent order, so long as the tribunal is only exercising its power granted by legislation – An order requiring the employer to provide a satisfactory reference will be outside the tribunal's terms of reference. However, even here it is possible to request a Tomlin Order staying the case for a set period while the parties give effect to their agreement.

Section 203(3)(a) ERA provides that the Settlement agreement must be in writing. The written document must fully set out the terms of the Settlement agreement. Where common law rights are being compromised in addition to statutory rights, then it is good practice for the terms of settlement of both claims to be incorporated into the same Settlement agreement. There is no requirement for the agreement to be in any particular format and the document can take the form of either a letter, deed or contract. The crucial point is for the agreement to contain the statutory requirements. However, a well drafted agreement will additionally cover many of the issues relevant to the employment relationship.

The Settlement agreement will usually be drafted by the employer or the employer's representative/solicitor. Many agreements follow a standard format and the temptation is to follow a standard WP precedent. Care should be taken when adopting this practice, as the terms of each agreement should be unique to the individual employee who is the subject matter of the agreement.

Section 203(3)(b) ERA provides that the Settlement agreement must relate to the particular proceedings. An agreement made within actual proceedings must relate to those proceedings. Where a

Settlement agreement is reached on the basis of anticipated proceedings, such proceedings should be specified.

Relevant cases include, In Hinton v University of East London and Wilson v Stockton-on-Tees Borough Council. Consequently the employer should always exercise care when attempting to settle future claims. Any waiver of future claims should be clear and unambiguous. The employee should be invited to enter into a warranty, to the effect that the employee is not aware of any such future claims. A general waiver will not be adequate.

Section 203(3)(c) ERA states that an employee must receive independent legal advice, from a relevant independent advisor, about the Settlement agreement and in particular its effect on the employee's ability to pursue rights before an ET. If not, then there will be a problem with enforceability. For the purposes of the above an adviser is defined as falling into one of the following categories;

1. a qualified lawyer.
2. A duly authorised officer, official, employee or member of an independent trade union.
3. a duly authorised employee or volunteer at an advice centre.
4. a person of a description specified in an order made by the Secretary of State.

Section 203(3)(d) ERA provides for indemnity insurance on the part of the professional advisor. At the time of the advice there must be in force a contract of insurance provided for members of a profession or professional body. This insurance or indemnity should cover the risk of a professional indemnity claim.

The effect of s203(3)(d) ERA is that an additional layer of protection is provided in favour of the employee, in the event of negligent advice being provided by the relevant adviser. In contrast to the applicable employment tribunal time limits for presentation of a statutory claim, the limitation period for negligence is six years.

Section 203(3)(e) ERA provides that the Settlement agreement must identify the adviser. The name and address of the adviser must be written into the agreement. In Lambert v Croydon College (1996) a settlement agreement failed to state the name of the legal adviser. However it was clear from the surrounding correspondence who the adviser was. Nevertheless, the tribunal held that the agreement had failed to comply with the conditions under s203(3)(e).

This is the extent to which the adviser should be identified. The adviser should avoid becoming a party to the agreement, and this might happen in circumstances where the agreement requires the adviser to execute the agreement as an additional party. In such situation, any warranties given in the agreement may also bind the additional party.

Where the adviser signs the agreement on behalf of a party, it should not be taken for granted that the adviser has authority to enter into the agreement on his/her client's behalf. In this situation a prudent adviser should obtain confirmation from his/her opponent's adviser, that such authority has been provided.

In Gloystarne & Co Ltd v Martin (2001) IRLR 15 the claimant's trade union representative purported to settle an employment tribunal claim on the claimant's behalf. The EAT held that the settlement was not binding on the basis that the representative had not been properly authorised by the claimant to enter into such an agreement, and that the representative did not have ostensible authority to bind his client.

Section 203(3)(f) ERA provides that the agreement must specify that the conditions regulating Settlement agreements are satisfied. This is effectively a declaration in the body of the agreement confirming that the statutory requirements have been complied with. The case of Palihakkara v British Telecommunications plc (2006) is relevant.

As previously indicated the effect of a valid Settlement agreement will be to waive an individual employee's rights. Once the agreement has been executed the Settlement agreement is enforceable by either party.

Arguments based on duress are often rejected by the courts. In Sphikas & Son v Porter (1997) the EAT defined this as a combination of pressure and the absence of practical choice. In Hennessy v Craigmyle & Co Ltd (1986) although the CA was prepared to accept the proposition that tribunals do have the power to set aside an agreement on common law grounds, they refused to do so in this case. As far as the CA was concerned, economic pressure in itself did not amount to duress.

Misrepresentations are statements which induce a person to enter a contract. Fraudulent misrepresentation has a common law action for in the tort of deceit, that is statements made with no belief in there truth. Secondly an action for a negligent misrepresentation lies; under the Misrepresentation Act 1967 which gives civil remedies where a person has made a statement without reasonable care. Finally an action also lies for an innocent misrepresentation under the Misrepresentation Act 1967 which allows rescission in lieu of damages (to establish the position before a contract was made) this is where untrue statements are made innocently.

Arguments based on misrepresentation have had more success, particularly where it has been found that one of the parties has acted in bad faith, misrepresented the true position or adopted unfair method in concluding a compromise agreement. In Industrious Ltd v Horizon Recruitment Ltd (in liquidation) & anor (2009), the EAT held that tribunals have jurisdiction to determine whether or not a settlement agreement is unenforceable because of misrepresentation.

Chapter 11 – Conclusion

It is suggested that a significant problem affecting the ETR is the engagement of the same set of rules regardless of the subject matter in dispute. The ETR adopts a one size fits all approach, regardless of whether the dispute is for a simple wage claim or complex discrimination case. There is no mechanism to distinguish between types of claim.

Hence an unrepresented employee seeking to recover outstanding wages of £100, must abide by the same rules of procedure as a represented applicant seeking to recover future loss of earnings. Although the ET members may treat the same differently, the ETR are identical for each Claimant. The civil courts are different. A civil claim can be allocated to either the small claims court, fast track or multi-track.

This deficiency has been recognised by the Gibbons Review, which recommended the introduction of a new process to deal with simple monetary disputes without the need for an ET hearing. It is submitted that this recommendation does nothing to resolve a significant flaw of the ETR, namely, that the rules are unnecessarily complex and act as a deterrent to access by the unrepresented litigant.

The complexity of employment legislation is such that there will always remain a requirement for detailed rules of ET procedure in order to govern the conduct of a dispute. Some are highly critical of the growth of workplace legislation on the basis that such expansion did not necessarily go hand in hand with access to justice. To quote Cicero, "the more laws, the less justice".

There appears to be a shift in the UK from the old voluntary system of industrial relations, to one of tight legal regulation and individual employment rights. Whereas 30 years ago, membership of a trade union enabled workers to collectively enforce rights directly with their employer, an employee is now more likely to have to secure his workplace rights on an individual basis.

However, the expansion of individual employment rights requires access to an appropriate forum in which to enforce those rights. It is submitted that in its present form, the ETR act as an inhibitor to access, especially if the employee is unrepresented.

Gibbons recommended the simplification of employment law. This may be possible with regard to unfair dismissal, but it is difficult to see how simplification can be attained in respect of many discriminatory employment rights which emanate from European Directives.

The simple truth is that employment legislation is substantially different to that which existed at the time of Donovan. The Donovan ethos is no longer attainable because it is not practical. A complex discrimination claim cannot be resolved in the type of forum originally suggested by Donovan.

On this basis, it is suggested that a significant proportion of the ETR should be preserved. Modification should be concentrated on how to deal with different types of claim. A straight forward unfair dismissal or other type of claim should be allocated to an appropriate track, which would be dealt with in an expeditious manner and governed by an easily comprehensible and user friendly procedure. Costs encourage lawyers, and lawyers, (whether intentionally or otherwise), increase formality. Hence there should be no scope for costs, other than claims which are obviously vexatious or unreasonable.

Complex employment cases, or claims over a certain value, should be allocated to an appropriate multi-track. A detailed set of procedural rules would be inevitable in order to achieve appropriate resolution of the issues in dispute. Here, legal representation would be of benefit, and should be encouraged in order to facilitate ET access. Costs should be recoverable, and Legal Aid made available.

The allocation of a claim to an appropriate track works in the civil courts, and there is no reason why the same principle cannot be applied in the ET.

Gibbons suggested the application of early case management. He additionally suggested an early quantification of the Claim. Both recommendations being eminently sensible, not only to weed out weak cases, but also to identify complex and large claims at an early stage, so that appropriate ET resources can be properly targeted.

Some view the promotion of mediation facilities as a method of resolving a contentious discrimination issue, yet at the same time preserving the working relationship where there has been no dismissal.

Gibbons considered that fundamentally what is required is a culture change, "so that the parties to employment disputes think in terms of finding ways to achieve an early outcome that works for them, rather than in terms of fighting their case at tribunal". To this end, Gibbon's recommendation of abolition of the Statutory dispute resolution procedures and their replacement with alternative forms of pre-commencement dispute resolution, is a step in the right direction.

It is submitted that a separate labour court is an important component in a modern industrialised society. Most industrialised economies possess a distinctive and specialist forum for the resolution of workplace disputes. Examination of the ETR, has shown that on the whole, the ET plays a central role in the resolution of workplace disputes. In this regard it has fulfilled the function which Donovan originally envisaged.

Bibliography

PUBLICATIONS

Deakin, S. and Morris, J. Labour Law (5th Edition). Hart Publishing: Oxford.
Selwyn, N. Law of Employment (16th Edition). Oxford University Press: Oxford.
Brennan, T., Smith, I. and Randall, N. (1996 -) Harvey on Industrial Relations and Employment Law. LexisNexis, Butterworths: London.
Korn, A. and Sethi, M. Employment Tribunal Compensation (3rd Edition). Oxford University Press: Oxford.
Kidner, R. Blackstone's Statutes on Employment Law (15th Edition). Oxford University Press: Oxford.
Cunningham, N. Employment Tribunal Claims – Tactics and Precedents (1st Edition). Legal Action Group: London.
Lewis, T. Employment Law – An Adviser's Handbook (7th Edition). Legal Action Group: London.
Holland, J. and Burnett, S. Employment Law (2nd Edition). Oxford University Press: Oxford.
Taylor, N. Guide to the Professional Conduct of Solicitors (8th Edition). Law Society Publishing: London.
Yew, J. Dismissals – Law and Practice (2nd Edition). Law Society Publishing: London.
Manley, I. and Heslop, E. Employment Tribunals – A Case Management Guide (1st Edition). Law Society Publishing: London.
Scrope, H. and Barnett, D. EmpLaw Professional. Disclaw Publishing Ltd: York.

JOURNALS AND ARTICLES

Macmillan, J. (Mar 1999) Employment Tribunals: Philosophies and Practicalities, ILJ 1999.28(33).

Citizens Advice Bureau: (Oct 2006) Response to the Draft Tribunals, Courts and Enforcement Bill, Linskell, R. (Jan 2007).

Stuck in the 20th Century, Employment Lawyers Association, ELA Briefing, Vol 14(1), 4.

Salter, M. (Dec 2006) Choose your Court – Forum Shopping in Discrimination Cases, Solicitors Journal, Vol 150(47), 1588-1589.

Veale, S. (1998) "Tribunals", Tribunals 1998, 5(2), 19.

Lewis, R. and Clark, J. (Sept 2000) Arbitration in Dismissal Disputes.

Dolder, C. (Dec 2004) The Contribution of Mediation to Workplace Justice, 33 Indus.L.J. 320.

Hepple, B. and Morris, G.S. (Sept 2002) The Employment Act 2002 and the Crisis of Individual Employment Rights, ILJ 2002.31(245).

Chapman, C. (May 2004) Employment Tribunal Reforms - An Integral Part of Workplace Dispute Resolution or an Economy Measure?

Underwood, K. (Aug 2004) Procedure Round-Up, Emp Law & Lit 9.8(12).

Yew, J. (Sept 2006) Ambulance Chasing and Wasted Costs, 156 NLJ 1344.

Latreille, P.L. (Dec 2005) Making a Difference? Legal Representation in Employment Tribunal Cases, ILJ 2005.34(308).

Moher, J. (May 2004) Law and Industrial Relations – Too much Law, Too many Lawyers? Industrial Law Society lecture.

Meeran, G. (Summer 2006) The Wider Principle, Judicial Studies Board – Tribunals.

GOVERNMENT REPORTS

Report of the Committee on Administrative Tribunals and Enquiries: 1957 Cmnd 218, Sir Oliver Franks.

Royal Commission on Trade Unions and Employers Associations 1965-1968: Cmnd 3623, Lord Donovan.

Tribunals for Users. One System, One Service. Report on the Review of Tribunals: (March 2001), Sir Andrew Leggatt.

Moving Forward; The Report of the Employment Tribunal System Taskforce: (July 2002), Janet Gaymer.

Employment Regulation; Striking a Balance – Report of the Cabinet Office Better Regulation Taskforce: (May 2002), David Arculus.

A Review of Employment Dispute Resolution in Great Britain: (March 2007), Michael Gibbons, DTI/Pub 8512/2k/03/07/NP.

Success at Work – Resolving Disputes in the Workplace: (March 2007), DTI/Pub 8513/1k/03/07/NP.

GENERAL REPORTS AND REVIEWS

Annual Report of the Council on Tribunals 2003/04.

Employment Tribunal Service Annual Report and Accounts 2005-2006: (July 2006).

Employment Lawyers Association: (May 2006), ELA Employment Tribunal Monitoring Survey 2006, ELA Briefing Vol 13, (Special Edition).

The Law Society (Oct 2006), Dispute Resolution Survey - Statutory Dispute Resolution Procedures.

Lord Chancellor's Dept Press Release 106/03: (March 2003), Government Announces Modernised Tribunals Service.

ACKNOWLEDGMENTS

Contains public sector information licensed under the Open Government Licence v3.0.

www.nationalarchives.gov.uk/doc/open-government-licence

www.ingramcontent.com/pod-product-compliance
Lightning Source LLC
Chambersburg PA
CBHW070232180526
45158CB00001BA/437